1st EDITION

Perspectives on Modern World History

The Korean War

1st EDITION

Perspectives on Modern World History

The Korean War

Myra Immell

Editor

GREENHAVEN PRESS
A part of Gale, Cengage Learning

Detroit • New York • San Francisco • New Haven, Conn • Waterville, Maine • London

Elizabeth Des Chenes, *Managing Editor*

© 2011 Greenhaven Press, a part of Gale, Cengage Learning.

Gale and Greenhaven Press are registered trademarks used herein under license.

For more information, contact:
Greenhaven Press
27500 Drake Rd.
Farmington Hills, MI 48331-3535
Or you can visit our Internet site at gale.cengage.com.

For product information and technology assistance, contact us at
Gale Customer Support, 1-800-877-4253.

For permission to use material from this text or product, submit all requests online at
www.cengage.com/permissions.

Further permissions questions can be e-mailed to permissionrequest@cengage.com.

Articles in Greenhaven Press anthologies are often edited for length to meet page requirements. In addition, original titles of these works are changed to clearly present the main thesis and to explicitly indicate the author's opinion. Every effort is made to ensure that Greenhaven Press accurately reflects the original intent of the authors. Every effort has been made to trace the owners of copyrighted material.

Cover image copyright © Bettman/Corbis and © Keystone Pictures USA/Alamy.

LIBRARY OF CONGRESS CATALOGING-IN-PUBLICATION DATA
The Korean War / Myra Immell, book editor.
    p. cm. -- (Perspectives on modern world history)
    Includes bibliographical references and index.
    ISBN 978-0-7377-5794-1 (hardcover)
    1. Korean War, 1950–1953. 2. Korean War, 1950–1953--United States. I. Immell, Myra.
    DS918.K5637 2011
    951.904'2--dc22

                                                                            2011005912

Printed in the United States of America
1 2 3 4 5 6 7 15 14 13 12 11

CONTENTS

assistance for South Korea and the unprecedented response of the United Nations to that request.

CHAPTER 2 Controversies Surrounding the Korean War

in which he and the other members of his Korean division took part.

FOREWORD

"History cannot give us a program for the future, but it can give us a fuller understanding of ourselves, and of our common humanity, so that we can better face the future."
— *Robert Penn Warren,*
American poet and novelist

The history of each nation is punctuated by momentous events that represent turning points for that nation, with an impact felt far beyond its borders. These events—displaying the full range of human capabilities, from violence, greed, and ignorance to heroism, courage, and strength—are nearly always complicated and multifaceted. Any student of history faces the challenge of grasping the many strands that constitute such world-changing events as wars, social movements, and environmental disasters. But understanding these significant historic events can be enhanced by exposure to a variety of perspectives, whether of people involved intimately or of ones observing from a distance of miles or years. Understanding can also be increased by learning about the controversies surrounding such events and exploring hot-button issues from multiple angles. Finally, true understanding of important historic events involves knowledge of the events' human impact—of the ways such events affected people in their everyday lives—all over the world.

Perspectives on Modern World History examines global historic events from the twentieth-century onward by presenting analysis and observation from numerous vantage points. Each volume offers high school, early college level, and general interest readers a thematically arranged anthology of previously published materials that address a major historical event, with an emphasis on international coverage. Each volume opens with background information on the event, then presents the controversies surrounding that event, and concludes with first-person narratives from people who lived through the event or were affected by it. By providing primary sources from the time of the event, as well as relevant commentary surrounding the event, this series can be used to inform debate, help develop critical thinking skills, increase global awareness, and enhance an understanding of international perspectives on history.

Material in each volume is selected from a diverse range of sources, including journals, magazines, newspapers, nonfiction books, personal narratives, speeches, congressional testimony, government documents, pamphlets, organization newsletters, and position papers. Articles taken from these sources are carefully edited and introduced to provide context and background. Each volume of Perspectives on Modern World History includes an array of views on events of global significance. Much of the material comes from international sources and from US sources that provide extensive international coverage.

Each volume in the Perspectives on Modern World History series also includes:

- A full-color **world map**, offering context and geographic perspective.
- An annotated **table of contents** that provides a brief summary of each essay in the volume.
- An **introduction** specific to the volume topic.
- For each viewpoint, a brief **introduction** that has notes about the author and source of the viewpoint, and that provides a summary of its main points.
- Full-color **charts**, **graphs**, **maps**, and other visual representations.

- Informational **sidebars** that explore the lives of key individuals, give background on historical events, or explain scientific or technical concepts.
- A **glossary** that defines key terms, as needed.
- A **chronology** of important dates preceding, during, and immediately following the event.
- A **bibliography** of additional books, periodicals, and websites for further research.
- A comprehensive **subject index** that offers access to people, places, and events cited in the text.

Perspectives on Modern World History is designed for a broad spectrum of readers who want to learn more about not only history but also current events, political science, government, international relations, and sociology—students doing research for class assignments or debates, teachers and faculty seeking to supplement course materials, and others wanting to improve their understanding of history. Each volume of Perspectives on Modern World History is designed to illuminate a complicated event, to spark debate, and to show the human perspective behind the world's most significant happenings of recent decades.

INTRODUCTION

Q: *"Mr. President, everybody is asking in this country, are we or are we not at war?"*
A: *"We are not at war."*

Q: *"Mr. President, would it be correct . . . to call this a police action under the United Nations?"*
A: *"Yes. That is exactly what it amounts to."*
— *June 29, 1950, president's news conference*

The above quotes are from US president Harry S. Truman's news conference four days after the North Korean assault on South Korea and two days after the president sent American troops into battle as part of a United Nations peacekeeping force. Technically, the president was correct when he told reporters that the US presence in Korea was a "police action." Officially, it was never more than that because he never asked Congress for a formal declaration of war. But in actuality, unofficially, the United States was at war in Korea. It was one of more than a dozen nations caught up in a 1,127-day conflict that took the life of more than 33,000 Americans and in which more than 103,000 troops were wounded.

Because it fell between World War II and the Vietnam War, for many years the Korean War was "The Forgotten War" or "The Unknown War." Today those names do not ring so true. Over time the war and the people who fought to bring it to an end have been more fully acknowledged and recognized. In 1995, for example, forty-two years after an armistice was signed, US president Bill Clinton and South Korean president Kim

Young Sam dedicated a Korean War Veteran's Memorial in Washington, D.C., to the men and women who served during the conflict. More recently, on September 15, 2010, the sixtieth anniversary of the landing in Korea of the 1st Division Marines from Camp Pendleton, North Carolina, another memorial took place. US Marine Corps Commandant General James T. Conway formally dedicated on the Camp Pendleton base a granite Korean War battle monument in tribute to the more than 4,400 US marines and soldiers who did not survive the Battle of Chosin Reservoir. The memorial also honors those who survived the battle, as well as Korean War veterans, with the inscription, "We Few, We Chosin Few, We Eternal Band of Brothers."

Chosin Reservoir was just one of many battlefields during the three years of the Korean War. Inchon, the Pusan Perimeter, Old Baldy, and Pork Chop Hill were a few of the others. But most agree that none was as brutal as the Battle of Chosin Reservoir, fought from November 27 to December 13, 1950. In the view of a marine who fought in that battle, what made it different from other battles that had fierce fighting and many casualties was the intensely cold and harsh weather and the fact that he and his comrades were fighting off six Chinese divisions. Roy E. Appleman, a combat historian in Korea for the US army, summed up the hallmarks of the battle as "misery, soul-crushing cold, privation, exhaustion, heroism, sacrifice, leadership of high merit at times, but finally, unit and individual disaster."

The battle got underway when a US Marine division and British Marine Commandos, part of a United Nations force, pressing north in the Chosin Reservoir area were taken by surprise by a joint Chinese and North Korean force. Wearing quilted uniforms that blended in with the snow-colored ground, the Chinese divisions had clandestinely crossed the Yalu River into eastern North Korea. The American trucks, tanks, and artillery were noisy. The Chinese were not. They had pushed south stealthily and silently, moving during the night and keeping hidden during the day. They greatly out-numbered the United Nations forces and soon had them completely surrounded.

The United Nations forces fought fiercely under the most deplorable weather conditions. In a 2006 interview with HistoryNet.com staff, battle survivor Lee Bergee spoke of cold that dropped to minus 54 degrees. Below he describes the conditions the men had to endure in what became known as "Frozen Chosin":

> The water in our canteens froze. We had to work the operating handles on the breechblocks of our M-1 rifles every now and then so they wouldn't freeze shut. Beads of ice formed in our beards and in our nostrils, and some of the men had to get the corpsmen to chip the ice out of their noses. Standing watch, you stomped your feet constantly and wiggled your toes inside the shoepacs to keep the circulation going. The cold seeped through your clothing. . . . The wind hit your face until it was raw, and the driving snow whipped into your eyes and half-blinded you as you searched for enemy activity. You dreamed of being close to a roaring fire . . ."

Bergee goes on to relate how, in a frantic effort to get warm, he and a few others set a railroad boxcar on fire, climbed inside, and stayed there until they had no choice but to get out to escape the flames.

In the end, the United Nations forces ended up falling back to Hagaru, North Korea, at the southern end of the reservoir complex. The Chinese, however, kept attacking, which left the United Nations troops no choice but to begin a retreat south to the supply port of Hungnam on the Sea of Japan. Not ready to give up, they inflicted more than 37,000 casualties on the Chinese on their march out. From Hungnam, the wounded and the dead, as well as most of the equipment, were evacuated on naval ships, after which United Nations forces blew up the entire port facility.

Few would disagree with the following statement by a US marine who survived Chosin:

> The Battle of Chosin Reservoir ranks among three major epic battles of the Marine Corps, along with the battle of Bella Woods during World War I and the battle of Iwo Jima, World War II. This was one battle in which 17 Medal of Honors, 72 Navy Crosses, numerous Silver Stars and Bronze Stars were awarded, not to mention the untold number of Purple Hearts. The tactics used in the battle of Chosin are and have been studied in great depth in military schools. I have a Marine buddy who designed a bumper sticker that reads: "Once Upon a Time Hell Froze Over. We Were There."

The Korean War took a heavy toll—up to 5 million dead, wounded, or missing, half of them civilians. It was, in essence, the first shooting of the Cold War, the post-World War II attempt by the United States and the Soviet Union to gain world influence by means short of total war. It did prevent communism from spreading into South Korea, but, in the view of most historians, it led to little or nothing else. The combatants signed an armistice, but it was a truce and no more. There were no treaties and no official end to the war. North Korea remains a Communist stronghold and the reunification that both North and South Korea professed to be seeking remains elusive, with North Korea and South Korea two separate countries still divided at the 38th parallel. US troops still are stationed in South Korea and the truce between the two Koreas remains a controversial and uneasy one.

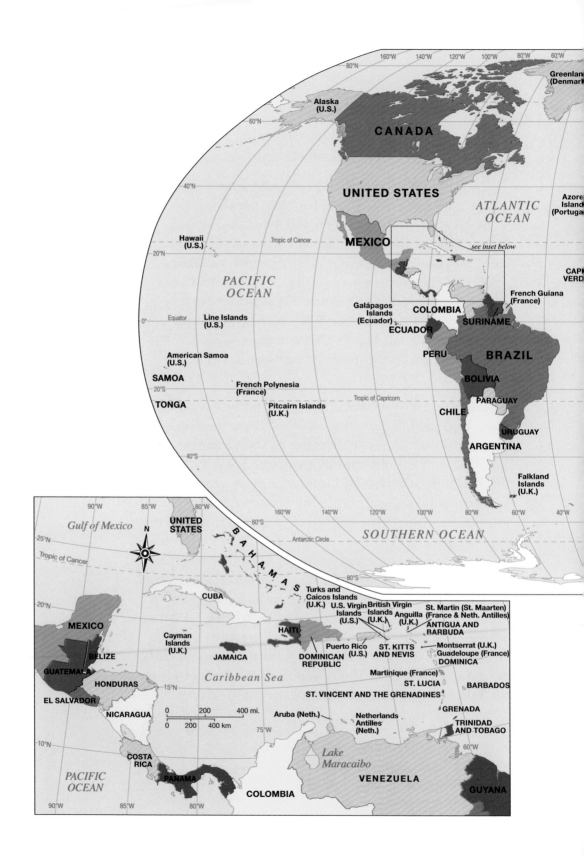

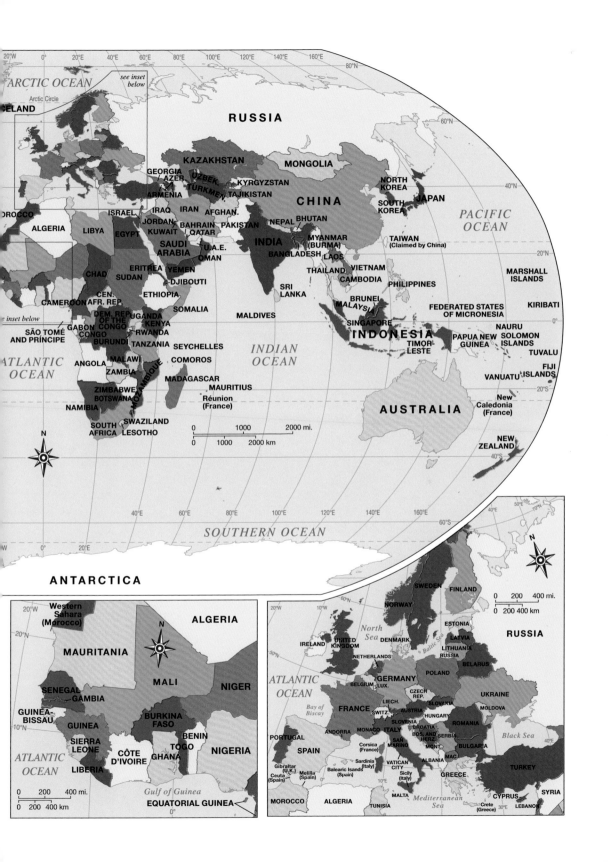

CHAPTER 1

Historical Background on the Korean War

The Korean War: An Overview

Judson Knight

The following viewpoint provides an overview of the events leading up to the Korean War, the conduct of the war, the circumstances that resulted in the dismissal of General Douglas MacArthur, and the war's aftermath and legacy. The conflict began as a civil war in 1950 with the North Korean invasion of South Korea, but its roots go back to World War II. It quickly escalated into an international conflict with a United Nations peacekeeping force supporting South Korea and Communist Chinese forces supporting North Korea. The war lasted three years and helped draw sharp lines between the West and the Communist world. It ended in a stalemate, with North and South Korea remaining two separate countries with opposing political philosophies. Judson Knight is a professional writer who has published more than a dozen books and contributed to hundreds of reference volumes.

Photo on previous page: Civilians flee south from US-occupied Pyongyang, North Korea, over a bombed bridge to escape the advance of Chinese Communist troops in December 1950. (**Max Desfor/AP Images.**)

SOURCE. K. Lee Lerner and Brenda Wilmoth Lerner, *Encyclopedia of Espionage, Intelligence, and Security.* © Gale, a part of Cengage Learning, Inc. Reproduced by permission. www.cengage.com/permissions.

Although it is often described as the "forgotten war," the conflict in Korea cost some 3 million lives over the course of three years, and helped set the tone for the larger Cold War. Both an international and a national conflict, the Korean War demonstrated the strengths and limitations of the United Nations (UN), and established the framework for the policy of containment that would lead the United States into the much longer conflict in Vietnam. Korea also solidified American attitudes toward communism, and reaction to events there served to influence both the rise of Senator Joseph McCarthy and the fear of communist "brainwashing." As much a war of intelligence as of arms, Korea saw the birth of the modern U.S. signals intelligence framework as the Armed Forces Security Agency (AFSA) gave way to the National Security Agency (NSA).

> By 1947, it had become apparent that Korea, in Japanese hands since 1910, would not easily be reunited under a non-Communist government.

In the end, an allied force of South Korean, American, British, Australian, and Turkish troops frustrated the aspirations of the North Korean Communist government, aided by the People's Republic of China, to control the Korean peninsula. The truce in 1953 established an uneasy framework—not quite war, not quite peace—that nevertheless remains in place [more than] half a century later.

Background to the Conflict

The roots of the Korean War . . . lay in World War II. Soon after 1945, the British and American alliance with the Soviet Union broke down in Europe, and the Korean hostilities brought the end of this partnership in Asia as well. The Soviets had fought World War II entirely on their western front, and only entered the Pacific war on a last minute bid for territory. . . .

Soviet dictator Josef Stalin's lack of participation in the Pacific theatre did not preclude his plans to extend the reach of Soviet Communism into that area. He was aided by an agreement with the United States that the Japanese would surrender to Soviet forces north of the 38th parallel on the Korean peninsula, which enabled him to establish a Communist government in Pyongyang [North Korea] under the leadership of Kim Il Sung. . . .

By 1947, it had become apparent that Korea, in Japanese hands since 1910, would not easily be reunited under a non-Communist government. Soon another event served to further raise the specter of Communist expansionism in Asia. In October 1949, the victory of [Chinese Communist] Mao Zedong's forces placed the world's largest population under the Communist rule of the People's Republic of China (PRC). Meanwhile, the United States had withdrawn its troops from Korea, and it now petitioned the UN to ensure free elections in Korea. The Soviets had withdrawn their troops as well, but refused to agree to these elections. On June 25, 1950, Kim's armies swept southward to unite the country by force.

The United Nations Acts

An emergency meeting of the UN Security Council resulted in a resolution to stop the North Korean assault. Though the Soviet Union was one of the five permanent Security Council members—along with the United States, United Kingdom, France, and the Republic of China—it had boycotted the meeting in protest of the U.S. effort to block the admission of the PRC. Because of their failure to show up at the Security Council meeting (a mistake they would not again repeat), the Soviets were unable to exercise their veto power against the American call for a "police action" on the Korean peninsula.

Although the Korean conflict is rightly called a war, there was no accompanying declaration by the U.S.

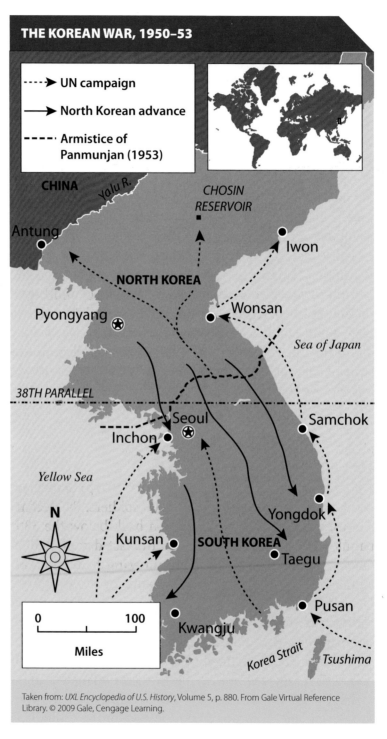

THE KOREAN WAR, 1950–53

- - - -▶ UN campaign

——▶ North Korean advance

- - - -· Armistice of Panmunjan (1953)

CHINA

Yalu R.

CHOSIN RESERVOIR

Antung

Iwon

NORTH KOREA

Pyongyang

Wonsan

Sea of Japan

38TH PARALLEL

Seoul

Samchok

Inchon

Yellow Sea

N

Yongdok

Kunsan

SOUTH KOREA

Taegu

0   100

Miles

Kwangju

Pusan

Korea Strait

Tsushima

Taken from: *UXL Encyclopedia of U.S. History*, Volume 5, p. 880. From Gale Virtual Reference Library. © 2009 Gale, Cengage Learning.

Congress; instead, President Harry S. Truman ordered U.S. troops into battle as part of a UN peacekeeping force on June 27, 1950. Four U.S. divisions landed on the Korean peninsula to join the South Korean forces there, but the North Koreans soon drove them all the way to Pusan, at the extreme southeastern end of the peninsula. Soon afterward, however, General Douglas MacArthur abruptly shifted the tide of the war by landing a massive force at Inchon, some 100 miles (160 km) south of the 38th parallel and well behind North Korean lines. He thus cut the North Korean army in two, and began moving northward, toward what now looked like an easy victory.

> The Communist force did not manage to move any further into South Korean territory, and thus began a lengthy stalemate that would characterize the remainder of the war.

As the UN forces moved toward the Yalu River, which separated North Korea from China, Beijing issued a stern warning that it would not look lightly on the presence of a hostile force just across the border. MacArthur, however, remained confident, and at Thanksgiving 1950 promised Americans that their sons would be home for Christmas. This was not to be, as on November 25 the Chinese People's Liberation Army swept across the border with a force of some 180,000 soldiers. By December 15, the allied forces had fallen back below the 38th parallel, and two weeks later, on the last day of 1950, a Chinese-North Korean force numbering half a million troops pushed into South Korea again.

MacArthur Takes a Stand

Thanks to relentless bombing by allied forces, the Communist force did not manage to move any further into South Korean territory, and thus began a lengthy stalemate that would characterize the remainder of the war. American leaders were sharply divided as to the means of resolving the conflict. MacArthur favored an extremely aggressive policy toward China, and proposed a naval blockade combined with bombing of Chinese bases in Manchuria. Truman, however, recognized the danger of such action, which he believed would bring a swift response from the Soviet Union. In the sharply polarized world climate, the price of aggression in Korea would almost certainly be armed conflict with the Soviets, and . . . the result could very well be nuclear war. . . .

Overstepping the bounds of his authority as a military leader, MacArthur called on the American people to support his war plans, and for this act of insubordination, Truman relieved him of duty on April 11, 1951. Replaced by General Matthew B. Ridgway, MacArthur returned to the United States a hero. . . . He would become a powerful symbol for the most extreme anti-Communist elements, who soon gained a voice in the Senate under the leadership of McCarthy. Thus began a sort of cold war within the Cold War, a division of the American public that would culminate with the bitter disagreements over the Vietnam War that emerged nearly two decades later.

> "In keeping with the emerging modern face of warfare, the Korean conflict was as much a battle of propaganda and intelligence as it was one of military forces."

Eisenhower and the War's End

Meanwhile, on July 10, 1951, the allied forces began a lengthy series of talks with the Communists. The situation remained unresolved during the 1952 presidential elections, and helped pave the way to victory for Republican presidential candidate Dwight D. Eisenhower . . . [who] opposed the Korean War, and vowed to end it.

Winning the presidency with the promise "I shall go to Korea," Eisenhower soon made good on his vow. . . . In private discussions with Chinese leaders he made it clear that he would take aggressive steps, up to and including the use of nuclear weapons, if the talks were not soon brought to resolution. Though fighting resumed briefly in June 1953, in the end Eisenhower's gambit won out, and on July 27, the two sides signed an armistice. Although the South gained possession of some eastern mountains north of the 38th parallel, the line virtually served as the boundary between North and South Korea.

A Battle of Propaganda and Intelligence

In keeping with the emerging modern face of warfare, the Korean conflict was as much a battle of propaganda and intelligence as it was one of military forces. Both sides took large numbers of prisoners of war (POWs), which they exchanged at the end of the fighting, and the Communists in particular made heavy use of the pro-paganda value to be gained from POWs. Eight different POW camps dotted a stretch along the Yalu River, and in these facilities the Communists sought to demoralize their captives by segregating them according to rank, nationality, and even race. They bombarded the POWs on a daily basis with lessons on the superiority of Com-munism over capitalism, but the purpose of these activi-ties seems to have been harassment rather than an actual effort to win converts.

The experience added a new term to the English language: brainwashing. The term referred to a variety of psychological and sometimes physical techniques intended to obliterate an individual's beliefs and replace them with new ones. Despite fears of brainwashing that spread through American society in the war's aftermath, there was never any conclusive psychological proof that brainwashing as such actually occurred. . . .

In the behind-the-scenes dimension of the Korean War, the success of allied efforts in signals intelligence (SIGINT) was much more firmly established than that of the Communists in brainwashing. . . .

In fact, the modern U.S. intelligence community had only barely come into existence at the war's outset, and Korea marked a turning point. Before the war, budgets for intelligence operations had been lean, but after the outbreak of hostilities, Washington made a much firmer commitment to its intelligence community. . . .

The Legacy of Korea

Some 37,000 Americans died in Korea, along with smaller casualties among the British, Australian, and Turkish forces. The North Koreans lost half a million soldiers, and the Chinese sustained losses of one million. By far the worst casualties belonged to the South Koreans, who lost 1.3 million civilian and military personnel. Though the war resulted in a stalemate, it preserved South Korean independence, and resulted in the establishment of boundaries that remained in place 50 years later.

The war helped draw sharp lines between the Communist world and the West, and in its immediate aftermath, Americans were confronted with the specter of not one but two Communist superpowers allied against them. . . .

As for the two countries whose conflict had drawn the world's attention, the war only solidified the division between them. For many years, South Korea would maintain a strict authoritarian regime that, while liberal in comparison to that of North Korea, was hardly so by modern standards. In the 1980s, however, it would emerge as an economic powerhouse, and as its populace prospered, they began to demand greater political options. In time, their nation would become an example of the relationship between economic and political liberalization.

By contrast, North Korea would serve to exemplify the disastrous consequences of strict totalitarian control in practice. An Orwellian state, it was the virtual kingdom of Kim, which he would pass on . . . to his son Kim

Photo on previous pages: A multinational force including US soldiers fought in the Korean War after the Communist north invaded the south, in what amounted to the first heated conflict of the Cold War. Flags of allied nations fly over the War Memorial in Seoul, South Korea. (Jung Yeon-Je/ AFP/Getty Images.)

Jong Il upon his death in 1994. Plagued by famine, unable to sustain even the most basic needs of its populace, North Korea survived on the remittances sent home by citizens living in Japan, and by arms sales to other rogue dictatorships. Its development of missile technology, which it exported to extremist regimes of the Islamic world, would earn it a place, along with Iran and Iraq, on the "axis of evil" described by President George W. Bush in 2002.

Communist Troops Move into South Korea

Times **(London)**

In the following article from June 26, 1950, a correspondent for the British newspaper the *Times* reports that early that morning North Korean troops had crossed into South Korea. The attack was totally unexpected and caught both the South Koreans and the United States by surprise. The South Korean president immediately appealed for help to the US State Department. The United States acknowledged the seriousness of the situation and reportedly alerted Japan-based General Douglas MacArthur to send whatever assistance possible from there. However, the newspaper reports that such action depended on a final go-ahead from US president Harry Truman. What impact the news from Korea would have on US policy in the Far East remained to be seen.

SOURCE. "Communist Troops Move into South Korea," *Times* (London), June 26, 1950. Copyright © 1950 Times Newspapers Ltd. Reproduced by permission.

Troops from North Korea crossed the 38th parallel into the Republic of Korea at several points early this morning and shortly after noon the North Korean wireless station at Pyongyang declared that a state of war had been effective since 11 A.M. But Dr. Syngman Rhee, the President of South Korea, is not accepting the broadcast as an official declaration.

President [Harry S.] Truman, who flew to his home at Independence, Missouri, yesterday, . . . at first decided not to return until to-morrow as originally planned, but at three o'clock this afternoon it was announced that he would leave by air within an hour.

The first news of the invasion reached Washington about 9 o'clock last night (equivalent to 11 A.M. June 25 by Korean time) and about an hour later confirmation was received from the United States Ambassador at Seoul [South Korea], Mr. John J. Muccio, who reported that the attacks were serious but that he was then unable to tell whether it was an all-out invasion. A meeting was held immediately in the State Department attended by Mr. Dean Rusk, Assistant Secretary of State for Far Eastern Affairs, Mr. John Hickerson, Assistant Secretary of State for United Nations Affairs, and Mr. Frank Pace, Secretary of the Army.

American Reaction to the South Korean Appeal for Help

The Korean Ambassador, Mr. John Myung Chang, called at the State Department in the early hours of the morning . . . to deliver an urgent appeal for help. It is understood that General MacArthur has been instructed to send whatever is possible from Japan, but no doubt a final decision on this matter awaits the President's return. Congressional approval is unnecessary in the early stages, as Korea is included in the Military Aid Programme and deliveries for some time can be covered in that way. But it is unlikely that Congressional approval

An Unexpected Assault, an Army Unprepared

There was nothing obscure or subtle about the North Korean invasion. . . . A heavy bombardment, followed two hours later by a spearhead of some 150 Soviet-built T-34-85 late-model medium tanks, and 110 warplanes, paved the way for the bulk of the Korean People's Army to surge across the [38th] Parallel in the most blatant—and one-sided—cross-border invasion since German panzers [tanks] had rolled into the Balkans in 1941. . . .

Still, the ROK [Republic of Korea] command was not alerted to an impending full-scale assault; because of previous engagements and artillery duels across the Parallel, this attack at first was generally seen as just another probe or exercise in belligerence. . . . The troops at the immediate front knew quickly enough what they were facing, but communication was not one of the strengths of the ROK Army. Not that prompt information would have made much of a difference. The ROK Army was anything but prepared to meet full-scale invasion. Five of its eight divisions were positioned several miles south of the Parallel. The Kaesong corridor, a wide, geographically featureless valley leading straight to Seoul without any natural barriers except for the Imjin River, was guarded by only one ROK division. The Uibongju corridor, also leading to Seoul, was, also, protected by a lone ROK division. . . . Half of the ROK Army was on leave, and numerous ROK civilian leaders were out of the country. . . . And it was a Sunday.

SOURCE. *Stanley Sandler,* The Korean War: No Victors, No Vanquished. *Lexington: University Press of Kentucky, 1999, pp. 49–50.*

would be withheld, as one or two members of Congress have already given their opinion that if South Korea is allowed to fall no small nation will feel safe and south-east Asia can be written off.

> Members of Congress have already given their opinion that if South Korea is allowed to fall no small nation will feel safe and south-east Asia can be written off.

Should the United States reach the point where direct intervention is considered necessary there is at present one carrier, two cruisers, and 10 destroyers in the Far East, five fighter groups on Guam (in addition to those on the Japanese islands), and General MacArthur has about 120,000 troops under his command.

An Attack Out of the Blue

Reliable news of the progress of the invasion has been difficult to get. According to reports so far an artillery bombardment began about 4 A.M., after which troops crossed the border at 11 points and at one point pushed three miles into South Korea before meeting with resistance. One report says that northern troops occupied the town of Kaesong near the border on the west, about 40 miles from Seoul, by 9:30 A.M. and there are also reports of a landing on the east coast as far as 40 miles south of the border.

The attack was quite unexpected. It has certainly taken the State Department by surprise and there has been, apparently, no intelligence report of the movement or concentration of troops which might have suggested preparations for an invasion. Also the rainy season is just starting, which made this an unlikely time to undertake a military adventure.

The American Presence in South Korea

There are something over 2,000 Americans in South Korea, where the Economic Cooperation Administration

[E.C.A.] has its biggest mission: there are 500 officers and men in the Korean military advisory group and over 1,000 officials of the United States Army, the State Department, and the E.C.A.—since the deterioration of the position of the Korean Government the E.C.A. has been progressively taking over more and more of the country's administration.

It was only last Wednesday that [former US Senator] Mr. John Foster Dulles left Seoul for Tokyo and before leaving he said that he had been told that the Communists had been spreading rumours that Korea might be left alone in the defence of its freedom. He added: "I hope the days I have spent here will be one more evidence of the fact that Korea does not stand alone."

Mr. [Louis A.] Johnson, the United States Secretary of Defence, and General [Omar] Bradley, chairman of the United States Joint Chiefs of Staff, returned from their Far Eastern trip yesterday afternoon. Mr. Johnson said: "We have seen all our important commands in the Far East and I think we have got the facts." According to Tokyo reports the facts they have collected lead them to agree with General MacArthur that the United States must retain bases in Japan after a peace treaty is signed, and must take positive action to prevent the fall of Formosa to the Chinese Communists. However, both refused to comment until after they and Mr. John Foster Dulles, who is expected back in the middle of the week, have reported to the President. To what extent today's news from Korea will change their views and their recommendations remains to be seen.

Photo on previous page: South Korean troops, although outfitted with American trucks and hardware, were unprepared for invasion by North Korea in June 1950. (T. Lambert/AP Images.)

Events in Korea Lead to a Call for Action

Ferdinand Kuhn

The following viewpoint from the Washington Post reports on the outcome of the June 27, 1950, meeting of the United Nations Security Council. During the meeting, a majority of council members agreed to support a United States' resolution that recommended the United Nations help South Korea resist Communist North Korea's armed attack and invasion and reestablish peace and security. An alternative resolution that would renew the cease-fire order and get mediation underway between North and South Korea was proposed by Yugoslavia and rejected in favor of the US resolution. Ferdinand Kuhn was a staff writer for the Washington Post.

Embattled Korea can expect more than American ships and planes as a result of an unprecedented agreement in the United Nations [U.N.] Security Council today.

SOURCE. Ferdinand Kuhn, "Seven Countries Line Up Behind Washington in Quick Action," *Washington Post*, June 28, 1950. Copyright © The Washington Post. Reproduced by permission.

U.N. Approval of an American Resolution

Delegates of seven out of the 11 nations on the Council—enough for a majority—announced that they favored calling on all members of the U.N. to help Korea against the Communist invasion.

The seven said they would support an American resolution recommending:

"That the members of the United Nations furnish such assistance to the Republic of Korea as may be necessary to repel the armed attack and to restore international peace and security in the area."

A vote was delayed until 10 o'clock tonight to give the delegates of India and Egypt more time for instructions from home. But whatever the instructions may be, majority approval of the American resolution was certain.

> It will be the first time since the charter was signed . . . that the United Nations has asked for collective help to a victim of aggression.

A Historic Milestone

When the vote comes, it will be the first time since the charter was signed five years ago that the United Nations has asked for collective help to a victim of aggression.

The British are known to be anxious to send planes and perhaps small naval craft from their base at Hongkong. The Australians have already announced that they would contribute.

What other countries may decide, and what help they can give, was a matter of guesswork tonight. But it was clear that the United Nations had passed a historic milestone at the very moment when its fortunes seemed lowest.

The biggest crowd in U.N. history stormed the temporary headquarters at Lake Success [New York] to watch the proceedings. Officials estimated that 5,000

KOREAN WAR PARTICIPANTS

United Nations Forces	Communist Forces
Australia	China
Belgium	North Korea
Canada	Soviet Union
Colombia	
Denmark	
Ethiopia	
France	
Greece	
India	
Italy	
Luxembourg	
The Netherlands	
New Zealand	
Norway	
Philippines	
South Korea	
Sweden	
Thailand	
Turkey	
Union of South Africa	
United Kingdom	
United States of America	

Taken from: www.korean-war.com

visitors had been turned away after the council chamber had been packed to the doors.

The Soviet chair at the council table was empty all afternoon. Delegate Jacob A. Malik was not present to cast a veto or to delay the Council's action.

The American delegation had not been sure of Malik's intentions. One of the reasons President [Harry] Truman issued his statement this morning, instead of waiting for the Council to act, was the fear that Malik might return to the Council table just to throw a monkey-wrench into the machinery.

The United States' Position

The United States would have gone ahead with its Pacific plans in any event, an authoritative source said yesterday, even if Russia had interposed a veto. But as it turned out, the Security Council gave overwhelming backing to the Koreans and an equally emphatic indorsement of the American position.

> " The [UN] Security Council gave overwhelming backing to the Koreans and an equally emphatic indorsement of the American position. "

One delegate after another praised the President's statement, issued more than three hours before the Council assembled. Jean Chauvel of France expressed his country's "appreciation;" Sir Terence Shone of Britain called it a "forthright statement;" Delegate [Arne] Sunde of Norway said it was a "momentous" utterance.

Even T.F. Tsiang, representing Chiang Kai-Shek's Nationalist government [on Formosa, now known as Taiwan], expressed "gratitude" for the President's decision to protect Formosa with the American fleet.

"I think all my people must be grateful for that offer of aid," Tsiang said, although he insisted that Formosa had been a province of China before 1895 and must be regarded as such today.

A UN Security Council vote only days after the North Koreans' invasion of South Korea assured Western nations' participation in the struggle. **(Keystone/ Getty Images.)**

The U.N. Deals Swiftly with Aggression in Korea

In claiming Formosa for China, Tsiang was raising a legal issue that may plague the U.N. later in the year, when it faces the question of Chinese representation. But this was an issue for the future; the issue today was aggression in Korea, and the Security Council moved with unaccustomed speed in dealing with it.

The chairman, Sir Benegal Rau of India, began on a sober note.

"The events of the past two days," he said, "have filled all of us with the gravest anxiety as to the near future. Many see in them the beginning of a third world war with all its horrors.

"A terrible burden therefore rests upon us as the body charged with the primary responsibility for the maintenance of international peace. The people of the world are weary of war and rumors of war, and we must try our best not to fail them."

The Indian then recalled the "paralyzing distrust" and bitterness between India and Pakistan earlier this year, and the meeting between the prime ministers of the two countries that eased the tension. If this was intended as a hint of a Truman-Stalin meeting, the Indian did not make it explicit.

"I mention this by way of showing," he said, "that even when things appear to be at their worst there is no need for despair."

> [US ambassador to the U.N.] Warren R. Austin . . . described the Korean crisis as the gravest in U.N. history, and branded the invasion of Southern Korea as 'an attack on the United Nations itself.'

The United States' Argument

After inviting Ambassador John M. Chang to take his place for Korea at the end of the table, Rau called on Ambassador Warren R. Austin to speak for the United States. Austin described the Korean crisis as the gravest in U.N. history, and branded the invasion of Southern Korea as "an attack on the United Nations itself."

He argued that it was the Council's "plain duty" to invoke "stringent sanctions" to stop the attack, and said he was "happy and proud to report that the United States is prepared, as a loyal member of the United Nations, to furnish assistance to the Republic of Korea."

He then read the proposed American resolution, describing it as the "logical next step" after the cease-fire order of last Sunday. He also read President Truman's statement of a few hours before.

An Alternative Is Proposed and Ignored

The first to reply was Alex Bebler of Yugoslavia, who proposed a substitute resolution that would do no more than renew the cease-fire order and start mediation between the two governments in Korea. Bebler pictured the war in Korea as the consequence of the artificial division of the country along the thirty-eighth parallel.

A policy of "spheres of influence," he warned, could lead to a third world war, and he insisted that after only two days of fighting it would be wrong "to abandon all hope" of a settlement.

Ambassador Chang, speaking next for Korea, took no notice of the Yugoslav proposal, and pleaded with the Council to back its moral judgment of last Sunday "with the power of enforcement." He appealed for the help of all U.N. members "in order to expel the invader from our territory and act directly in the establishment of international peace and security."

Heavy Support for the US Resolution

A procession of speakers followed, all denouncing the invasion and supporting the American resolution. Chauvel of France said "the attack must be halted," and pledged the unreserved approval of his Government for the American stand.

Shone of Britain said the Security Council simply could not let its authority be flouted any longer. The British delegate incidentally denied "insinuations"—the source of which he did not identify—that his Government had been hesitant in the Korean crisis.

The delegates of Cuba, Norway and Ecuador all insisted that the Security Council must act quickly and boldly. At this point, to the disappointment of the 1,200 spectators, the debate was interrupted, first for an hour and then for a further three hours, while the Indians and Egyptians sought instructions by transocean phone.

A Legendary General Is Dismissed over US Policy in Korea

Gettysburg Times

In the following viewpoint from 1951, a Pennsylvania newspaper reports on the dismissal of General Douglas MacArthur from his positions as supreme allied occupation commander in Japan, United Nations (UN) commander-in-chief for Korea, United States commander-in-chief for the Far East, and commanding general of the US Army in the Far East. President Harry S. Truman attributed the dismissal to MacArthur's unwillingness to unconditionally support the Truman administration's and United Nations' policies on Korea and to public actions MacArthur took in an effort to change those policies. The decision to fire MacArthur was not an easy one. On one hand, officials feared that, because MacArthur was so popular with the public and had such strong political backing, dismissing him might split the country. On the other hand, they were afraid that not dismissing him might divide the UN coalition, which feared MacArthur would involve the United States in a major war in the Far East.

SOURCE. "Truman Fires Doug MacArthur," *Gettysburg Times*, April 11, 1951. Copyright © The Gettysburg Times. Reproduced by permission.

> 'General of the Army Douglas MacArthur is unable to give his wholehearted support to the policies of the United States government and of the United Nations in matters pertaining to his official duties.'

President Harry S. Truman fired Gen. Douglas MacArthur today on grounds he failed to support—and publicly sought to change—the grand strategy of the United Nations [U.N.] war against Red aggression in Korea.

In a sensational statement released at the White House at 1 A.M. this morning after days of soul-searching and indecision the President announced:

"With deep regret I have concluded that General of the Army Douglas MacArthur is unable to give his wholehearted support to the policies of the United States government and of the United Nations in matters pertaining to his official duties."

MacArthur Loses Four Important Positions

Acting with lightning speed on that conclusion once he had reached it, the President:

1. Relieved the 71-year-old MacArthur of his four-fold duties as supreme Allied occupation commander in Japan; United Nations commander in chief for Korea; United States commander in chief for the Far East; and commanding general of the United States Army in the Far East.

2. Named Lieut. Gen. Matthew B. Ridgway, field commander in Korea, to succeed MacArthur in all these commands. That means Ridgeway not only will direct the U.N. campaign in Korea but also wind up the Japanese occupation, assuming peace treaty plans go through.

3. Named Lieut. Gen. James A. Van Fleet, commander of the Second Army at Fort George G. Meade, Md., to take over the Eighth Army command in Korea from Ridgway.

4. Issued a set of secret messages exchanged between MacArthur and the joint chiefs of staff here. The evident aim was to show that MacArthur had scorned successive Washington directives to clear anything he had said on major political or military policy with either the State or Defense Departments.

A Major Difference of Opinion on US Far East Policy

The order relieving MacArthur of command was Mr. Truman's answer to the general's persistent campaign of public statements to get the United States to follow a different policy in the Far East and especially, with its U.N. allies, in the Korean War.

Essentially he has advocated expanding the war to include direct attacks on Red China. He has presented Asia rather than Europe as the critical theater of conflict with aggressive communism.

His dismissal amounts to reaffirmation by Mr. Truman of United States policies for a strictly limited war in Korea, if possible, and for treating Europe as the ultimately decisive area of contest with Soviet Communist power.

The bombshell announcement was made by Press Secretary Joseph H. Short at a hastily summoned White House news conference.

The President told MacArthur he is free to "travel to such places as you select"—thus freeing the general to return to this country after an absence of nearly 14 years. There were immediate demands in Congress that he come to Washington to give his views.

A Damning Exchange of Orders and Messages

In addition to the heretofore secret messages, orders sent out shortly before midnight to bring about the spectacular shakeup in the Far East were also released.

The secret message file showed MacArthur had been covered in a general presidential order last Dec. 6, clamping down on policy statements by all government officials. He had been bluntly reminded of this by Mr. Truman's direction on March 24, after issuing his famous bid to the Red commander in Korea to talk peace as U.N. forces reached the 38th parallel [the dividing line between North and South Korea].

Meanwhile, on March 20, the record showed MacArthur had sent to House Republican Joe Martin (Mass.) the letter endorsing Martin's idea of using Chinese Nationalist troops on Formosa [now Taiwan] to open a "second front" against Red China, and adding his own conviction that Asia rather than Europe is the critical theater of conflict with world communism. Martin released the letter last week.

There was also an exchange of messages between the joint chiefs of staff and MacArthur on the question of arming Korean troops. This showed MacArthur raising a serious question whether more Koreans should be armed in view of weapons needs for the developing Japanese police.

Thus the White House sought to meet a MacArthur statement last week-end that the recent release of 120,000 South Koreans from military units was the result of a policy decision made in Washington and beyond his power to control.

Two Decisive Events

While the Truman administration's feud with MacArthur goes back many months, two events apparently were decisive in bringing on the showdown. One was the

Photo on following page: General Douglas MacArthur (left) made statements about the Korean War that were contrary to policy set by President Harry Truman (right). **(MPI/Getty Images.)**

general's 38th parallel statement, in which he not only invited Red peace talks but also implied the United Nations might alter their policies and attack Red China.

This set tempers rising in Allied capitals here and abroad. For not only did the policy makers have no intention of expanding the war but, as the messages now released show, they were planning their own much less belligerent bid to peace. Once MacArthur had spoken this was scrapped.

The second incident was the MacArthur letter to Martin. Martin is a leader of the President's Republican opposition; he used the letter in attacking the Presidentially sponsored universal military training bill in the House.

That was last Thursday. Almost immediately Mr. Truman began conferring with Secretary of Defense Marshall Gen. Omar Bradley, chairman of the joint chiefs of staff, and other advisers on whether he should fire MacArthur and if so, how. . . .

> 'It is fundamental . . . that military commanders must be governed by the policies and directives issued to them in the manner provided by our laws and constitution.'

It is authoritatively understood that either the President or Secretary of State [Dean] Acheson, perhaps both, may now follow up with public statements or speeches designed to clarify Korean war aims and restate the limits and direction of American policies in Korea.

Dealing with a Terrible Dilemma

The President rejected suggestions, which had been given wide currency yesterday, that for the time being he adopt a middle course—between the extremes of ignoring what MacArthur had done or firing him. He evidently preferred the view of some of his most responsible advisers that he was caught in a terrible dilemma from which he could remove himself only by a major operation.

The nature of the dilemma, as privately described by these officials, was this: MacArthur had shown by ignoring several directives that he did not intend to stop publicly preaching his ideas. But what he was advocating was contrary to United States government policy. He has enormous public prestige and strong political backing. If he was fired, it might split the country; but if he was not fired it might split the U.N. coalition, which was afraid MacArthur would get the United States in a big war in the Far East.

The Importance of Sticking to Orders

Britain has been particularly sensitive about MacArthur's statements because British leaders cling to the hope that the Chinese Communists will listen to reason and negotiate a peace. But Canada and other countries have been almost equally critical of the man who exercised command over their troops.

Hence in the statement in which he set forth in official language the reasons for his action, Mr. Truman laid heavy stress on the requirement, as he sees it, that military commanders stick to their orders.

"Full and vigorous debate on matters of national policy," the statement said, "is a vital element in the constitutional system of our free democracy. It is fundamental, however, that military commanders must be governed by the policies and directives issued to them in the manner provided by our laws and constitution. In time of crisis, this consideration is particularly compelling."

Praise and Censure Combined

Then the President paid tribute to the general:

"General MacArthur's place in history as one of our greatest commanders is fully established. The nation owes him a debt of gratitude for the distinguished and exceptional service which he has rendered his country in posts of great responsibility. For that reason I repeat my regret at the necessity for the action I feel compelled to take in his case."

The combination of praise and censure in the President's statement has been characteristic of his relations with MacArthur, especially since the Korean War started last June.

The Mightiest Blow of the Korean War

Sam Summerlin

In the following viewpoint from the August 29, 1952, issue of the Canadian newspaper the *Lethbridge Herald*, Sam Summerlin describes the air raids carried out by United Nations allied bombers on the North Korean capital of Pyongyang. North Koreans were warned ahead of time about the raid by Radio Seoul, and leaflets were dropped on the capital city advising civilians to leave the area. The raids went on relentlessly from sunrise to sundown. They enveloped the city in smoke and caused massive damage as hundreds of planes loosed tons of gallons of flaming gasoline and high explosives on dozens of targets and sprayed the area with thousands of rounds of machine-gun bullets. Among the many targets were more than forty vital military targets on the outskirts of the city, including airfields, a power plant, factories, supply dumps, and troop barracks. Sam Summerlin served as a news correspondent during the Korean War.

SOURCE. Sam Summerlin, "Pyongyang Is Blasted by Waves U.N. Bombers," *Lethbridge Herald*, August 29, 1952. Copyright © The Lethbridge Herald. Reproduced by permission.

Planes from four Allied countries today hit Pyongyang, capital and largest city of Communist North Korea, the mightiest blow of the war. The reeling city was wrapped in great clouds of smoke and torn by explosions.

A Record Number of Sorties

Three waves of land and carrier-based fighter bombers bombed and strafed the big Red [Communist] nerve centre in a record 1,403 sorties, or individual flights, the United States Fifth Air Force and Navy said.

Black smoke poured from the factories, supply dumps and troop billets at the outskirts of Pyongyang, forewarned of the raids by radio and leaflets.

The hundreds of tons of weapons UN allies dropped on Pyongyang also included a military "joke" in the form of an actual kitchen sink. (AP Images.)

A returning United Nations pilot said the city "was blowing up all over."

Planes from three U.S. aircraft carriers off the east coast of Korea flew 210 sorties over the Red capital.

Allied Planes Pour It On

Some 420 planes poured 4,000 gallons of flaming gasoline and 597 tons of high explosives on more than 40 Communist targets during the dawn-to-dusk raids. They sprayed 52,000 rounds of machine-gun bullets on the area, the air force said.

Until today, the biggest single air blow of the war had been July 11, when more than 500 fighter bombers and Superfortresses poured 1,400 tons of bombs on Pyongyang during 1,063 sorties.

Today's first wave of jet and prop-driven planes battered Communist anti-aircraft defences, which pilots said threw up a heavy curtain of flak. Other waves concentrated on stockpiles, barracks, industries and airfields used to bolster the Communist war effort.

Raids Silence Pyongyang Radio

Pyongyang radio was off the air, and monitors in Tokyo said it still had not come on for its regular broadcasts tonight.

Allied air raids have driven Pyongyang radio from the air waves twice recently. Once was in June, when a smashing blow at the Suiho hydro-electric power plant on the Manchurian frontier cut off the capital's power. The second was the big July 11 raid.

South African, South Korean and Australian planes joined U.S. pilots in this fifth attack of the Red capital since Aug. 1.

Bombers Inflict Major Damage

In the morning smash alone, 420 fighter bombers strafed and hurled 100 tons of bombs at two airfields, a power

> More than 500 bombers hurled 1,400 tons of bombs on [Pyongyang] July 11 [1950], in the greatest single air blow of the war.

plant, factories, anti-aircraft batteries, and some 40 other vital military targets at the outskirts of the city that had a population of 342,000 in 1942.

Four large explosions ripped the area after the bombs hit.

In the afternoon, 345 planes went back to hit the Reds again.

The air force said the first two waves of fighter bombers destroyed 42 and damaged 32 buildings, knocked out 20 gun emplacements, damaged a road bridge, scored two direct hits on a factory and cratered two airstrips.

U.S. jets moved in first to knock out the anti-aircraft batteries surrounding the targets. Then the fast jets unleashed their 1,000 pounders on the choice targets.

South Korean and South African pilots flying propeller-driven Mustangs joined the big air assault. Navy and Marine flyers flew Panther jets and prop-driven Corsair and Skyraider bombers.

Allied air losses, if any, were not announced.

The U.S. air force said jet fighters protecting the bombers shot down one Russian-built jet and damaged two other Red MIG's [jet fighter planes designed in the Soviet Union] in dogfights at 40,000 feet.

Pyongyang Received Advance Notice

Radio Seoul warned of the raid in advance, and leaflets were dropped on Pyongyang urging noncombatants to leave.

More than 500 bombers hurled 1,400 tons of bombs on the Red capital July 11, in the greatest single air blow of the war.

The mud-caked battlefront continued relatively quiet. For a week rain has kept the ground front a quagmire and fighting has been light across the 155-mile front.

The Korean War Ends in an Uneasy Truce

Independent Record

In the following viewpoint, a Montana newspaper announces that on July 27, 1953, a compromise armistice—that is a truce rather than peace—was signed regarding the Korean War. The article reports that, almost immediately after the signing, the Communist Chinese claimed victory in the war and put their soldiers on alert for any troublesome actions by United Nations (UN) forces. South Korean president Syngman Rhee expressed his lack of faith in the armistice, predicting that it would only lead to more war, and indicated that South Korea would honor it for "a limited time." The UN commander, American general Mark Clark, made it clear that, armistice or no, UN troops would remain in Korea. In accordance with the terms of the armistice, the exchange of more than 85,000 allied, North Korean, and Communist Chinese prisoners of war was scheduled to get underway.

SOURCE. "UN Commander, Red Generals Sign Armistice Document Ending War: Enemy Radio is Claiming Great Victory," *Independent Record*, July 27, 1953. Copyright © The Independent Record. Reproduced by permission.

Generals of the UN [United Nations] command and the Red [Communist] armies signed Monday [July 27, 1953] at long last a compromise armistice in the bitter, three-year Korean war. It means not peace but a nervous truce.

A hush fell suddenly across the battlefront 12 hours after the truce was signed. But almost until the final minute Communist and Allied guns roared in thunderous barrages.

The two generals signed in 10 minutes a document that was two years and 17 days in the writing.

Warnings of an Uneasy Truce

Hardly had they completed the signing when these ominous, clashing warnings were sounded:

The Chinese Red Peiping radio boasted that the Communists had won "a glorious victory" and cautioned Red soldiers to remain "highly vigilant and guard against any disruptive actions from the other side."

UN Commander Gen. Mark Clark told his troops flatly there will be no "immediate or even early withdrawal" from Korea and declared that the UN is staying on—"a reminder to the enemy and his emissaries that our might and power stand behind the pledges of the United Nations to defend the Republic of Korea against any aggressor."

> The 8th army commander, Gen. Maxwell D. Taylor, said the armistice was 'just a suspension of hostilities, which may or may not be preparatory to permanent peace.'

South Korean President Syngman Rhee declared again his conviction that the armistice "will prove to be the prelude to more war . . . more suffering and ruin . . . further Communist advances by war and subversion." He said South Korea would not disturb the truce for "a limited time" while a political conference tries to unify the country and work out plans for withdrawal of Chinese Communist forces from the North.

The 8th army commander, Gen. Maxwell D. Taylor, said the armistice was "just a suspension of hostilities, which may or may not be prepartory to permanent peace."

Signing of the Armistice

The brief signing ceremony at Panmunjom ran smoothly in sharp contrast to the months of sharp words, demands, counterdemands and walkouts that marked the long-drawn negotiations.

Without a word to each other, Lt. Gen. William K. Harrison Jr. signed for the Allies and Gen. Nam Il for the Communists in a bare, one room, Oriental type building hastily constructed by the Communists for the occasion.

The chief negotiators began penning their names 1 minute after the appointed hour of 10 A.M. and were through signing the 18 documents involved at 10:11.

Each looked at the other for a long moment after they were through. Nam Il arose from the table and walked out the north door. Harrison went out the south door.

Gen. Clark signed nine copies of the truce document at Allied advance headquarters in Munsan [South Korea] three hours later.

The nine other copies were sent to North Korea for signing by the Communist commanders. North Korean Marshal Kim Il Sung and Chinese Gen. Peng Teh-huai.

Tuesday morning the Reds will be handed the copies signed by Clark, and the UN command will receive the copies signed by Kim and Peng.

The Issue of Prisoners of War

The first big task ahead in the armistice is the exchange of prisoners. These include 3,313 Americans and about 8,000 South Koreans and 1,000 from other Allied nations held by the Reds, and 74,000 North Korean and Red Chinese held by the UN command.

The secret record of the negotiations, released after the signing, showed that the Reds hold 12,736 prisoners of war.

The exchange of prisoners who want to return home is expected to begin in a week or less.

The UN said about 7,800 North Koreans and 14,500 Chinese captives have said they do not want to return home and will be turned over to a repatriation commission composed of Switzerland, Sweden, Poland, Czechoslovakia and India.

India's troops will guard them in the buffer zone while Communist agents confer with them.

The Communists said they would return 300 prisoners a day, including sick and wounded. The UN command told the Reds it will turn back prisoners at the rate of 2,400 able bodied men daily, plus 360 sick and wounded.

A North Korean museum now occupies the land where a truce was signed between the north and south. Armed conflict might have ended, but hostilities continue until present day. **(Kim Jae-Hwan/ AFP/Getty Images.)**

Negotiating the Truce

If the Korean conflict was a strange new phenomenon for Americans, a half war in a world of half measures, negotiating their way out of it was even stranger. . . .

On July 8 [1953], when the first liaison teams met to work out details, the Americans had entered the hall and casually sat down, facing south. There was great consternation among the Communists, for it turned out that in Asia, the conqueror traditionally sat facing south; they had intended that the Americans sit facing north. When the full negotiating teams met two days later, the Communists had done their preparation rather better; they provided high chairs facing south for themselves, low chairs facing north for the United Nations [UN]. When the UN leader put a small flag on the table in front of him, the Communists bustled around and came in with a big flag to put on their side.

So it went; the Americans, extremely conscious of "oriental face," did their best not to make the Communists look like losers, and the Communists did *their* best to *make* the United Nations look like losers. Such little matters seemed almost laughable at first; unfortunately, they were symptomatic of the whole procedure. The American chief delegate, Vice Adm. C. Turner Joy, characterized the Communist negotiating style as insisting that two and two made six, and finally, after exhausting argument, conceding that it made five instead.

SOURCE: *James L. Stokesbury, A Short History of the Korean War. New York: William Morrow & Company, 1988, pp. 143–144.*

Policing of the Korean Truce Gets Underway

Sydney Morning Herald

The following viewpoint, from the August 3, 1953, issue of an Australian newspaper, focuses on the Korean armistice and the tasks of the two commissions and the Red Cross teams monitoring its observance. One commission's responsibility is the specifications, erection, and management of markers along the buffer zone. The other will take charge of the impending prisoner exchange to take place following a full-dress rehearsal of a processing system intended to return prisoners home as quickly as possible. United Nations Red Cross teams, made up of workers from the United States, South Korea, Denmark, Britain, Australia, Canada, Holland, the Philippines, and Turkey, are set to cross the Communist lines for the first time and greet the first groups of allied prisoners moving toward Panmunjom, North Korea. Communist and UN Red Cross workers will visit Communist-held allied prisoners and allied stockades in South Korea. A 10-person Red Cross coordinating group will remain at Panmunjom for the prisoner exchange.

SOURCE. "Start on Policing of Truce," *Sydney Morning Herald*, August 3, 1953. Copyright © The Sydney Morning Herald. Reproduced by permission.

The four-nation Supervisory Commission which will keep a watchful eye on observance of the armistice in Korea met for the first time yesterday [August 2, 1953] in an atmosphere of stiff formality.

Officers said later that conduct of the meeting was similar to the frigid atmosphere of the negotiations for the truce.

More than a half-century after war's end, prisoner swaps in the Korean Demilitarized Zone village of Panmunjom have given way to the return of remains. (Kim Jae-Hwan/AFP/Getty Images.)

The Supervisory Commission: A Call for Team Spirit

The delegates of the four neutral nations (Switzerland, Sweden, Poland, and Czechoslovakia) met in the "peace pagoda" at Panmunjom [on the border between North Korea and South Korea in the middle of the Demilitarized Zone (DMZ)] where the armistice was signed.

The Communist delegation included several Polish women, smartly dressed, with neat hair styles, and their faces thick with make-up.

After the Polish and Czech delegates had made short speeches, the chief Swedish delegate, Lieutenant-General Sven Grafstrom, urged the commission to work as a single body.

"In the English there is a phrase, 'team spirit,' and we hope that this will prevail in all our work." he said.

Peking (Communist) Radio said that the commission reached agreement on the specifications, erection, and supervision of markers along the 24-mile-wide buffer zone.

Teams of Allied and Communist officers will patrol the zone.

The Prisoner Exchange

The five-nation Repatriation Commission, which will supervise the exchange of prisoners, also met yesterday.

The exchange will begin on Wednesday, but the U.N. [United Nations] Command will hold a full-dress rehearsal to-morrow of a processing system designed to repatriate the men as quickly as possible.

The Communists announced that they will deliver Allied prisoners at a rate of 100 an hour for four hours each day, starting at 9 a.m. on Wednesday.

> The prisoner-exchange will bring home 12,763 Allied captives, including 3,313 Americans and 922 British. The Communists will receive in return 74,000 prisoners—69,000 North Koreans and 5,000 Chinese.

The Communists said that they wanted able-bodied prisoners returned to them before they got the sick and wounded.

The U.N. had proposed to hand over 360 sick P.O.W.s [prisoners of war] before the arrival of 2,400 able-bodied men on the first day.

The two sides were unable to agree on which side should be responsible for maintaining order in its own P.O.W. reception area. They decided to refer the question to the Military Armistice Commission.

The Exchange Role of Red Cross Teams

Red Cross teams will cross the Communist lines for the first time to-morrow and greet the first groups of Allied prisoners moving toward Panmunjom.

Peking Radio said that the first batch of non-Korean prisoners, who left the Communist camp at Pyoktong (on the North Korea-Manchuria border) yesterday, should arrive at Kaesong [North Korea] by train to-morrow.

Kaesong is the Communist advance truce headquarters north-west of Panmunjom.

These prisoners are believed to include men from Britain and the [British] Commonwealth.

The prisoner-exchange will bring home 12,763 Allied captives, including 3,313 Americans and 922 British. The Communists will receive in return 74,000 prisoners—69,000 North Koreans and 5,000 Chinese.

Thirty U.N. Red Cross workers will join 30 Communist counterparts in visiting the Allied prisoners in Communist hands. Thirty more will accompany an equal number of Communists to Allied stockades in South Korea.

A 10-man Red Cross coordinating group will remain at Panmunjom for the prisoner-exchange.

The U.N. group includes Red Cross workers from the United States, South Korea, Denmark, Britain, Australia, Canada, Holland, the Philippines, and Turkey.

The U.N. Red Cross teams will distribute cigarettes, towels, soap, shaving equipment, and toothpaste to Allied prisoners.

If the operation proceeds without a hitch, all Allied prisoners should be back in friendly hands 32 days after the first exchange.

The armistice terms are that the exchange must be completed within 60 days of the truce signing on July 27.

Evacuation Cheers and Handshakes

A special correspondent of the New China (Communist) news agency said that a bay near the prisoners' camp at Pyoklong became a little bustling harbour yesterday as a dozen barges and steam launches took repatriates to lorries [large trucks] on the opposite bank of the lake.

> The Communists had not relaxed their readiness for combat and the Allies must remain on the alert because of the possibility of incidents which the enemy could build upon.

There was much cheering and handshaking as the men, smartly dressed and carrying cakes and canned meat, embarked. Those not yet leaving lined the bank to wave good-bye.

As the boats moved out, some of the men began to play mouthorgans and guitars. British prisoners sang "Now is the hour."

Allied naval headquarters reported to-day that the Allies have completed the evacuation of islands which U.N. forces held off the east coast of Korea.

The truce terms provided that both sides would leave island territories behind the other's lines.

An Appeal by the US Secretary of State

The U.S. Secretary of State, Mr. John Foster Dulles, told Allied nations yesterday that President [Dwight] Eisenhower has approved a programme to use American forces in Korea to rebuild the country's roads, schools, and hospitals.

He urged the Allied Governments to consider using their forces the same way.

Mr. Dulles spoke at a private session of U.S. and foreign diplomats before his departure to-day for Korea on post-armistice political problems.

He said he hoped that the 15 other nations with units in the U.N. forces in Korea would keep them there.

The Communists had not relaxed their readiness for combat and the Allies must remain on the alert because of the possibility of incidents which the enemy could build upon.

Mr. Dulles said that the defense treaty he expects to negotiate with President Syngman Rhee would not prevent a later agreement on withdrawal of American troops from Korea, if that should prove desirable.

The Issue of Korean Unification

President Syngman Rhee said to-night that South Korea had agreed to postpone for a few months attempts to unify Korea while the Allies tried to reunify it by political means.

His statement was in reply to four questions which foreign correspondents submitted to him.

He said that Korea could not accept a truce until the Chinese were expelled from Korea. This would automatically reunite Korea.

"So long as the United Nations stands by its objective of the unification of Korea there won't be any reason for Korea to take unilateral action.

"If the United Nations should retreat from that, we should then face it alone."

CHAPTER 2

Controversies Surrounding the Korean War

The Soviet Union Is Mainly Responsible for the Korean War

Paul Wingrove

In this viewpoint, a British academic argues that responsibility for the Korean War lies primarily with Soviet leader Joseph Stalin. Because North Korea was a client state of the Soviet Union, North Korean leader Kim Il Sung had to have Stalin's agreement and support before he could wage war against South Korea. The author explains that Stalin was not in favor of the idea at first but soon changed his mind. It was Stalin who urged Kim to get the Communist Chinese involved, making it clear that their assistance was needed because the Soviet Union was not ready to get directly involved in Korean affairs. He contends that the war was not necessary and that Stalin miscalculated, damaging the interests of the Communist world. Paul Wingrove is a senior lecturer in politics at the University of Greenwich in the United Kingdom.

Photo on previous page: The Demilitarized Zone cuts the Korean peninsula into north and south at the 38th parallel. It is one of the most militarized borders in the world. (**Kaku Kurita/Time & Life Pictures/Getty Images.**)

SOURCE. Paul Wingrove, "Who Started Korea?" *History Today*, vol. 50, no. 7, June 30, 2000. Copyright © History Today. Reproduced by permission.

On June 25th, 1950, Communist North Korea launched an invasion across the 38th Parallel into South Korea. Initially taken aback, the West, under American leadership, quickly recovered and within days had obtained United Nations Security Council agreement to repel the attack. For [US] President [Harry S.] Truman this was a decisive encounter. As he saw it, North Korea's Communist leader Kim Il Sung was not acting independently, nor was the aim of this attack simply limited to reunification of the divided Korean peninsula. In this aggressive action he discerned the hand of the USSR [Soviet Union], and possibly that of Communist China. In Truman's words: 'The Reds were probing for weaknesses in our armour; we had to meet their thrust without getting embroiled in a worldwide war'. His Secretary of State, Dean Acheson, also concluded that 'it seemed close to certain that the attack had been mounted, supplied and instigated by the Soviet Union . . .', and:

> To back away from this challenge . . . would be highly destructive of the power and prestige of the United States . . . we could not accept the conquest of this important area by a Soviet puppet under the very guns of our defensive perimeter with no more resistance than words and gestures in the Security Council.

New Light on the Origins of the Korean War

Only recently, however, have the roles of [Soviet leader Joseph] Stalin and [Chinese Communist leader] Mao [Zedong] in unleashing the Korean War become better known, thanks to the opening of the archives of former Communist bloc countries. Researchers have also benefited from [Soviet] President [Boris] Yeltsin's personal decision in 1994 to present to the South Korean government hundreds of pages of high-level declassified documents relating to the origins of the war. Even so, the record is far from complete. In Russia many documents from the highly sensitive 'Presidential Archive' and from KGB [Soviet Committee for State Security] and military archives are simply not available, while China's archives are effectively closed to outsiders.

Nonetheless, fifty years on we are much clearer about the war's origins. Who wanted the war, and why? The answer seems to be that it was primarily Kim Il Sung who sought reunification of Korea through military action, but as a client state of the USSR he needed, and was given, the support and encouragement of Stalin. Kim was driven by the cause of reunification, but was also perhaps too easily impressed by Mao Zedong's successes in the Chinese civil war of 1946–49. Stalin came to see an attack on South Korea as a potentially cheap Cold War victory.

> 'The situation makes it necessary and possible to liberate the whole country through military means.'

Kim and Stalin: Differing Opinions on Reunifying Korea

Reunification through war seems first to have been raised as a serious possibility in March 1949 when Kim travelled to Moscow to meet with Stalin. Their exchange of March 7th is recorded as follows:

Kim Il Sung: We believe that the situation makes it necessary and possible to liberate the whole country through military means. The reactionary forces of the South will never agree on a peaceful reunification and will perpetuate the division of the country until they feel themselves strong enough to attack the North. Now is the best opportunity for us to take the initiative into our own hands. Our armed forces are stronger, and in addition we have the support of a powerful guerrilla movement in the South. The population of the South, which despises the pro-American regime, will certainly help us as well.

Stalin: You should not advance to the South. First of all, the Korean People's Army does not have an overwhelming superiority over the troops of the South. Numerically, as I understand, you are even behind them. Second, there are still American troops in the South which will interfere in the case of hostilities. Third, one should not forget that the agreement on the 38th Parallel is in effect between the USSR and the United States. If the agreement is broken by our side, it is more of a reason to believe that the Americans will interfere.

Kim Il Sung: Does it mean that there is no chance to reunify Korea in the near future? Our people are very anxious to be together again and to cast off the yoke of the reactionary regime and their American masters.

Stalin: If the adversary has aggressive intentions, then sooner or later it will start the aggression. In response to the attack you will have a good opportunity to launch a counterattack. Then your move will be understood and supported by everyone.

The Persistence of Kim Il Sung

Whatever his inclinations, Stalin was clear that this was not the time for military action. . . .

Kim was undeterred by Stalin's caution. . . . On September 3rd, 1949, [Soviet ambassador Terentii] Shtykov reported to Moscow that Kim had requested permission:

'If necessary, China has at its disposal troops which can be utilised in Korea.'

To begin military operations against the South, with the goal of seizing the Ongjin peninsula and part of the territory of South Korea to the east of the Ongjin peninsula. . . . Kim Il Sung considers . . . that if the international situation permits, they are ready to move further to the south. Kim Il Sung is convinced that they are in a position to seize South Korea in the course of two weeks, maximum two months.

Shtykov prudently counselled Kim that this question was 'very large and serious', and not to do anything until Moscow had considered the matter. Moscow, in the person of [Soviet deputy minister of foreign affairs] Andrei Gromyko, replied a week later, with instructions to the ambassador to 'give your evaluation of the situation and of how real and advisable is the proposal of our friends', indicating some change in Stalin's policy following the US withdrawal. After consultations in Pyongyang the Soviet chargé d'affaires, [Grigory] Tunkin, reported back to Moscow on September 14th that Kim had again indicated that he planned only a 'partial' operation on the Ongjin peninsula, with the possibility of moving further south if this attack resulted in 'demoralisation' of the enemy forces. Irrespective of the scope of Kim's plans, Tunkin stated that he personally remained unconvinced of the ability of the north to carry out an invasion, or to contain the war:

> The northern army is insufficiently strong to carry out successful and rapid operations against the south. Even taking into account the help which will be rendered to the northern army by the partisans and the population of South Korea it is impossible to count on a rapid victory. Moreover, a drawn out civil war is disadvantageous for the north both militarily and politically. . . . After their lack of success in China, the Americans will probably intervene more decisively than they did in China. . . .

Kim's Unflagging Commitment

Despite his over-optimistic expectations of the population of the south, Tunkin's assessment was sound. The message to Kim, formally delivered from the Soviet Politburo [principal policy-making body] on September 24th, reflected this judgement:

> It is impossible to acknowledge that a military attack on the south is now completely prepared for and therefore from the military point of view it is not allowed.

Yet Kim remained committed to his plans. In mid-January 1950, at a rather emotional lunchtime meeting, he told Shtykov:

> Lately, I do not sleep at night, thinking about how to resolve the question of the unification of the whole country. If the matter of the liberation of the people of the southern portion of Korea and the unification of the country is drawn out, then I can lose the trust of the people of Korea.

Kim then:

> Placed before me [Shtykov] the question, why don't I allow him to attack the Ongjin peninsula, which the People's Army could take in three days, and with a general attack the People's Army could be in Seoul in several days.

Stalin's Change of Mind

Shtykov replied that Kim should put such questions to Stalin personally, and reported this conversation to Moscow. In the event, an emboldened Stalin informed Shtykov in January 1950 that he agreed to a second meeting with Kim, now hinting at his new view of things:

> I understand the dissatisfaction of comrade Kim Il Sung, but he must understand that such a large matter in regard to South Korea as he wants to undertake needs large preparation. The matter must be organised so that there would not be too great a risk. If he wants to discuss

this matter with me then I will always be ready to receive him. Transmit all this to Kim Il Sung and tell him that I am ready to help him in this matter.

From now until the outbreak of the war on June 25th, 1950, Stalin encouraged Kim and armed him in preparation for an attack on the South. Why this change of heart? Partly because US troops had departed, but also because the 'international situation' had changed in a number of ways advantageous to the Communist world. According to a document prepared by Soviet Communist Party officials which summarised the second Stalin-Kim talks, held in April 1950, Stalin reasoned that

The Chinese Communist Party's victory over the Guomindang [Nationalist Party of China] has improved the environment for actions in Korea . . . if necessary, China has at its disposal troops which can be utilised in Korea . . . the Chinese victory is also important psychologically . . . [and] now that China has signed a treaty of alliance with the USSR, Americans will be even more hesitant to challenge the Communists in Asia . . . Such a mood is reinforced by the fact that the USSR now has the atomic bomb.

> 'Comrade Stalin added that the Koreans should not count on direct Soviet participation in the war because the USSR had serious challenges elsewhere to cope with, especially in the West.'

The Need to Involve China in Korean Affairs

Having decided that US intervention was unlikely, Stalin now made clear what would happen if, against his expectations, the war should spread:

Comrade Stalin added that the Koreans should not count on direct Soviet participation in the war because the USSR had serious challenges elsewhere to cope with, especially in the West. He again urged Kim Il Sung to consult with Mao Zedong and mentioned that the Chinese leader had a good understanding of Oriental matters. Stalin repeated that the USSR was not ready to get involved in Korean affairs directly, especially if Americans did venture to send troops to Korea.

Kim's argument had always been that American intervention was unlikely and that the war would be short. From a more calculated perspective, Stalin had come to accept this view, while taking precautions against the event of a different outcome.

Given that China was to play such a crucial role in the war, it is surprising that these Moscow-Pyongyang interactions were largely hidden from Mao. While some writers suggest that Stalin and Mao may have discussed

Although Mao Zedong (backdrop, center) backed North Korea's Kim Il Sung (left) in invading South Korea, Kim acted only after approval from Joseph Stalin (right). **(Park Ji-Hwan/AFP/Getty Images.)**

Korea during the latter's visit to Moscow from December 1949 to January 1950, this was almost certainly not the case. Indeed, in a telegram from Stalin to Shtykov sent in February 1950 Stalin commanded that:

> The question he [Kim] wants to discuss with me must be completely confidential. It should not be shared with anyone even in the North Korean leadership, as well as the Chinese comrades. . . .

Reluctant Agreement by Mao Zedong

Mao did not discover what was afoot until May, following Kim's month-long visit to Moscow in April. On Stalin's suggestion, Kim had travelled to Beijing [China] to see Mao to lay out his plans. While Mao and Kim were in talks [Soviet foreign minister] Andrei] Vyshinsky . . . informed Mao that Stalin had already agreed to Kim's 'proposal', and hinted at a role for Beijing:

> In a conversation with the Korean comrades Filippov [Stalin] and his friends expressed the opinion that, in light of the changed international situation, they agree with the proposal of the Koreans to move toward reunification. . . . In this regard a qualification was made . . . that the question should be decided finally by the Chinese and Korean comrades together, and in case of disagreement by the Chinese comrades the decision on the question should be postponed until a new discussion.

> "Stalin . . . initially pretended he was not involved in the war—a ploy that dismayed Kim and failed to deceive the West."

Thus, China was to be tied into the war, if only loosely. Mao gave a rather lukewarm agreement to Kim's plans, although for Kim this was sufficient. . . . This meeting, which ended with Mao's muted approval for the enterprise, cleared the way for June 25th attack.

An Appeal for Help

The North's invasion turned out to be spectacularly successful for the period that it took the West to recover, re-group and send troops to Korea. Stalin, taken aback by a United Nations intervention which confounded his calculations, initially pretended he was not involved in the war—a ploy that dismayed Kim and failed to deceive the West. [US general Douglas] MacArthur's bold execution of the landings at Inchon in September turned the tide, producing heavy defeats for the North Koreans. In a ciphered telegram of September 30th, Kim pleaded with Stalin:

> This was an unnecessary war, for which the responsibility lies mainly with Stalin.

If the enemy does not give us time to implement the measures which we plan, and, making use of our extremely grave situation, steps up its offensive operations into North Korea, then we will not be able to stop the enemy troops solely with our own forces. Therefore, dear Josif Vissarionovich, we cannot help asking you to provide us with special assistance. In other words, at the moment when the enemy troops cross the 38th Parallel we will badly need direct military assistance from the Soviet Union.

This, of course, was at odds with Stalin's intentions. Fortunately, Kim went on to request the formation of 'volunteer units in China and other countries of people's democracy', a request Stalin was only too eager to assist with. He immediately fired off a message to Mao:

If in the current situation you consider it possible to send troops to assist the Koreans, then you should move at least five-six divisions towards the 38th Parallel at once.

The War's Impact on China

As Stalin had always intended, he was not going to pull North Korean chestnuts out of the fire; the Chinese would undertake that task. In later years Mao recalled that it was only when the Chinese had proved their mettle in combat in Korea that Stalin lost some of his earlier suspicion of them. But this was no comfort for Mao, for not only did the Korean war involve huge sacrifices for his country, it also put off indefinitely the higher priority—the conquest of Taiwan.

This was an unnecessary war, for which the responsibility lies mainly with Stalin. His miscalculation damaged the interests of the USSR and the Communist world in general, and it is not surprising that upon his death in 1953 his successors quickly sought a formal end to the conflict. Nor is it surprising that Mao Zedong held a rather jaundiced view of the man who had armed the North for this war, permitted it to be launched, then expected others to save the day.

General MacArthur Did Not Deserve to Be Fired During the Korean War

Alexander Wiley

In this 1951 speech, a US senator speaks out against the dismissal of General Douglas MacArthur. He argues that MacArthur is a great leader—an American icon—and that firing him will have major consequences. In his opinion, President Harry Truman acted prematurely without making an effort to find another way to deal with MacArthur. Furthermore, he argues, the administration has been unfairly maligning MacArthur and misinterpreting his actions, because MacArthur did not deliberately defy higher authority and is not frivolously toying with a third world war in Asia. He asserts that based on MacArthur's many years of military experience, the General knows when the military should take the offensive. Alexander Wiley was a Republican US senator from Wisconsin.

SOURCE. Alexander Wiley, "Speech on the Firing of MacArthur," *Congressional Record*, April 17, 1951. U.S. Government Printing Office.

A great crisis in American and world politics has arisen. It has been precipitated by the Chief Executive [President Harry S. Truman] of our country in his firing of a great soldier, statesman, administrator, patriot—Douglas MacArthur. . . .

When Harry Truman sacked this great leader he was not simply removing a brigadier general or a captain down the line, he was removing a man who has become the world-wide symbol of America's fighting greatness, of our strength and courage, a man . . . who has carved for himself a niche in American history which is virtually unique. He removed a man who was not only the commander of our forces, but those of 52 other nations.

> There has been a great deal of bunk and baloney put out by the administration within the last four or five days in its puny attempt to justify the dismissal action.

Surely, if the President felt that his differences were so intensely strong with MacArthur and that some decision was necessary, surely a better way could have been found. Further consultation could have taken place between our Chief Executive and the United Nations [UN] commander. Instead, the President chose to take an action whose repercussions are so staggering that we can only barely perceive them now. . . .

Three Unjust Allegations Against MacArthur

There has been a great deal of bunk and baloney put out by the administration within the last four or five days in its puny attempt to justify the dismissal action. I want to analyze point by point some of the smears and phony inferences that have been made; some of the innuendoes that have been cast against General MacArthur; some of the misinterpretations that have been made of his position.

Now, first, is it true as administration supporters say, that MacArthur has willfully flouted higher authority? I say "No."

As has been documented from MacArthur head-quarters in Tokyo, the general is firmly convinced that he complied with the letter and spirit of the directives sent to him by Mr. Truman and by the Joint Chiefs of Staff. As a soldier, as former Chief of Staff, as a man who has been subject to discipline all his life and who has necessarily imposed discipline, MacArthur knows the necessity for obedience to one's superiors. He is not a man who lightly dismisses higher authority. . . .

Second, I want to point out that the administration's supporters would have us erroneously believe that Mac-Arthur was lightly toying with a third world war in Asia. I think that such a charge is absurd. Douglas MacArthur has seen the horrible results of war. He carries the scars of battle on his body. He has seen enough combat to know that war is a bloody, sickening affair. He knows that war, of itself, solves nothing.

Third, the administration's supporters contend that Douglas MacArthur, by urging the bombing of Man-churian bases, would bring on a full-scale war with Red [Communist] China. Well, my friends, according to the latest reports, there are over a half million Red Chinese troops posed for a spring offensive against the some three hundred thousand UN troops. If that is not a full-scale war, what is? . . .

The Validity of MacArthur's Policy

There are those who contend that MacArthur wants us to fight endlessly on the Asiatic continent. Well, we seem to be fighting endlessly on the Korean Peninsula and, ac-cording to geographers, that is still a part of the Asiatic continent.

But let me further point out this, my friends: Ear-lier this week the question was asked in the Senate, Has

General MacArthur ever stated that he wants to land an American army on the Asiatic continent? No supporter of the administration could answer that question by proving that MacArthur ever made any such a recommendation.

But I ask you . . . what would you do if you were in MacArthur's shoes and you saw the Red Chinese forces building up for their spring offensive? Would you keep your hands tied behind your back, so to speak, or would you want to send bomber formations up so as to stop the Red offensive before it started?

What I am driving at is this, my friends: Douglas MacArthur, with all his years of military background,

President Truman fired "the world-wide symbol of America's fighting greatness" in stripping General Douglas MacArthur of command. **(Fotosearch/Getty Images.)**

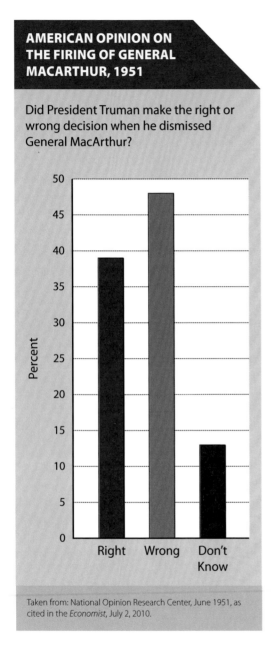

AMERICAN OPINION ON THE FIRING OF GENERAL MACARTHUR, 1951

Did President Truman make the right or wrong decision when he dismissed General MacArthur?

Taken from: National Opinion Research Center, June 1951, as cited in the *Economist*, July 2, 2010.

knows that the best time to stop an attack is to hit it before it is in a position to hit you. What's wrong with that policy? Nothing.

Playing Partisan Politics

And so, we could go on, answering point by point the smears against MacArthur. The situation boils down to the fact that the American people have faith in Douglas MacArthur, just as they lack faith in the Democratic administration. On the other hand, the administration lacks faith in Douglas MacArthur just as it lacks faith in the American people.

It is quite clear that the Democratic Party has been handling this MacArthur situation with the November 1952 election in mind. I say that it is up to the Republican Party to realize that to a tremendous extent the 1952 decision is at stake in how the MacArthur situation is handled. But I want to make myself perfectly clear.

I don't feel that we can become so exclusively absorbed in partisan politics and angles that we forget that infinitely more important than the welfare of our party is the welfare of our country. In this instance it is my firm judgment that a victory for the Republican Party in November 1952 is imperatively necessary for the future peace, prosperity, and freedom of America.

President Truman Had Reason and the Right to Fire General MacArthur

Julie A. Miller

In the following viewpoint, Julie A. Miller argues that President Harry S. Truman had a constitutional right—and the authority—to fire General Douglas MacArthur for insubordination. MacArthur's challenge to the president's role as the definitive voice of the nation's foreign policy had to be addressed. The Truman administration followed a policy of containment and was committed to fighting a limited war in Korea. Because MacArthur did not agree with Truman's policies, he publicly tried to influence those policies, thus violating his first duty: to obey the orders of his superiors. MacArthur persisted even though as a longtime military officer he knew that his role was to carry out US policy in Korea and not to involve himself in questioning the policy, especially not publicly. At the time this viewpoint was written, Julie A. Miller was a student at the United States Marine Corps Command and Staff College in Virginia.

SOURCE. Julie A. Miller, "Truman or MacArthur: Who's in Command?" CSC 1992. www.GlobalSecurity.org.

The President is responsible for conducting foreign policy for the United States. Explicit with the President's conduct of foreign policy are his roles as Chief Diplomat and Commander-in-Chief, concomitant is his authority to recall a recalcitrant general. During the Korean War two voices espoused policy for the U.S.: President [Harry S.] Truman and General [Douglas] MacArthur. This dichotomy of policy had to be resolved and eventually was with the dismissal of MacArthur. The conflict between Truman and MacArthur involved MacArthur's challenge to Truman's aforementioned roles: essentially a challenge to civilian control of the government in foreign affairs. Truman was clearly within his constitutional authority as the sole voice of foreign policy in the U.S. Government to relieve General MacArthur as Commander-in-Chief of the Far East. With the barrage of criticism leveled at Truman, most Americans at the time did not understand that his position was a constitutional one dealing with the insubordination of a theater commander. The decision was based on a thorough examination of MacArthur's proposals and his non-acceptance of their rejection by the Truman Administration. Larger issues of foreign policy and civilian control were at stake and had to be preserved at the relative minor expense of a subordinate.

> MacArthur did not seem to appreciate the fact that military factors had to [be] subordinated to political considerations with which he did not agree.

Limited War vs. Total War

Generally, Truman followed a policy of containment. This policy had worked in Turkey, Iran, and Greece, and Truman meant for it to work in Korea. The war had to be viewed in the context of possible repercussions with the U.S.'s allies and other foreign governments. Therefore, Truman pursued a policy of limited war in Korea. The

A General's Farewell to Congress

On April 19, 1951, General MacArthur addressed the US Congress about his dismissal and his perspectives on the political and military situation in Southeast Asia. It was his first trip to the United States since 1937. He concluded the speech—his last ever public appearance—with the following remarks:

I have just left your fighting sons in Korea. . . . It was my constant effort to preserve them and end this savage conflict honorably and with the least loss of time and a minimum sacrifice of life. Its growing bloodshed has caused me the deepest anguish and anxiety. . . .

I am closing my 52 years of military service. . . . When I joined the Army even before the turn of the century, it was the fulfillment of all my boyish hopes and dreams. The world has turned over many times since I took the oath on the plain at West Point. . . . But I still remember the refrain of one of the most popular barrack ballads of that day which proclaimed most proudly that—

"Old soldiers never die; they just fade away."

And like the old soldier of that ballad, I now close my military career and just fade away—an old soldier who tried to do his duty as God gave him the light to see that duty.

Good-by.

SOURCE. *General Douglas MacArthur, "The Address to Congress," as cited in Veterans of Foreign Wars,* Pictorial History of the Korean War. *Veterans' Historical Book Service, Inc. 1951, p. 383.*

concept of a limited war as opposed to total war was a political judgement of the conflict by civilian authorities and for political, not for military, objectives.

PERSPECTIVES ON MODERN WORLD HISTORY

The concept of limited war was new to Americans and to the military who were used to waging total war until a complete victory had been obtained. Wars were fought until the enemy was completely defeated and subjugated. In all previous wars this had been the case, especially in the so recently fought World War II. MacArthur's view was that war should be waged utilizing every means possible—totally—or war should not be waged at all. He had lots of support from the American public, as well as from some members of Congress, notably Senator [Robert A.] Taft and Representative [Joseph W.] Martin. MacArthur's views were given added credence because of his position as the local theater commander of the [Battle of] Inchon victory [of the Korean War], his prominence as the successful proconsul of Japan, his status as a war hero in the Pacific during World War II, and his exposure as a possible presidential nominee in 1948. He was thought to be almost an infallible authority on Far Eastern affairs—he had not set foot in the United States for fourteen years. . . .

Putting Military Factors Before Political Considerations

But the Korean War was not a total war, and a complete victory was not its goal. Korea was fought as a political war for political goals: initially to insure that the boundary at the 38th parallel would be maintained. (That policy was later changed to complete unification, but without success.) It was a limited goal and clearly within the framework of Truman's overall foreign-policy strategy. Korea was not the only factor Truman had to consider. It must be kept in mind that Truman's first priorities lay in Europe where the principle enemy was the Soviet Union—not Korea or China. He was much more concerned with building up the defenses in Western Europe and maintaining a cohesive NATO [North Atlantic Treaty Organization] alliance. Being an ardent

"Asia-firster," MacArthur was convinced that Communist China was the real enemy of the Western world, and the force behind the North Korean aggression. Of the relationship between Europe and Asia, MacArthur stated unequivocally that "here in Asia . . . the communist conspirators have elected to make their play for global conquest . . . that here we fight Europe's wars with arms while the diplomats there still fight it with words; that if we lose the war to communism in Asia, the fall of Europe is inevitable." MacArthur did not seem to appreciate the fact that military factors had to [be] subordinated to political considerations with which he did not agree. He publicly propagated policies that were directly opposed to Truman's. MacArthur advocated a four-point program that would have escalated the war and actively involved Communist China. His policy advocated a naval blockade of Communist China, unrestricted air and naval bombardment of Chinese military and industrial capacity, deployment of troops from Formosa [now Taiwan], and removal of all restrictions on the Nationalist Chinese troops to engage in diversionary attacks on the Chinese Mainland. His policies stressed the military factors which completely overshadowed the political implications so vital to Truman. The idea of a limited war was anathema to MacArthur's military mind. On this matter, he did not mince his words: "War never before in the history of the world has been applied piecemeal . . . that you wage half-war and not whole war is appeasement." MacArthur clearly did not or refused to understand that the limited war concept was specifically implemented to insure that the war did not escalate militarily to involve China and the Soviet Union in massive ground actions in Korea.

A Flagrant Case of Insubordination

The fact that MacArthur disagreed with the Truman Administration's foreign policy caused him to disobey his orders and try to seek a change over to his own policies. In disobeying his orders, MacArthur violated the first duty of a military man: to obey the orders of his superiors. A soldier can disagree with policy within the command structure on a private basis but not publicly. In the event that a soldier cannot carry out his orders, he is duty-bound to resign. There were no half-way measures to deal with insubordination without dire results politically and militarily. In this case, Truman would lose a brilliant military mind, as well as a popular figure, who, to date had basically supported his policies. When conducting a war, the Commander-in-Chief should not have to deal with an unsympathetic field commander at every juncture who cannot uphold policies in which he does not believe. Truman could not afford to continue placating MacArthur politically or militarily.

With MacArthur espousing contradictory policies at every turn, Truman had to deal diplomatically with the allies who were confused as to what the real policies were and who was actually making them. It was Truman's task to rally support for the United Nations' action and to explain the damage done to his credibility by MacArthur's statements. He was having a difficult time trying to maintain a consensus within his administration and with the Allies without having to constantly deal with MacArthur at every new turn. It is the job of the President as Chief Diplomat to deal with foreign governments. It is a political realm in which the military has no jurisdiction. Negotiations, settlements, peace initiatives, etc. are the prerogative of the President and his designated subordinates. After all, the whole purpose of diplomacy is to achieve goals without the use of military force. It was not MacArthur's right to present a virtual ultimatum to the North Koreans with unpleasant consequences if it were not heeded. That right clearly belonged exclusively to President Truman. And to make it more unpalatable to Truman was the fact that MacArthur's announcement,

Photo on following page: A soldier can disagree privately with orders from a superior, but to do so publicly—as General Douglas MacArthur (pictured) did—is insubordination. (Carl Mydans/Time & Life Pictures/Getty Images.)

labeled a "military appraisal," undermined and negated his own pending request for peace negotiations. In doing so, MacArthur ignored an executive order issued 6 December 1950 stating that all public statements be submitted for review first by the Defense or State Departments. It would have been less effective if Truman had gone ahead and issued his own statement and, at the same time try to discount MacArthur's. The damage to Truman's credibility had already been done.

The Issue of Control

Another point that must be considered is how much control the civil authorities can have over a local field commander without hampering the accomplishment of the military objectives. Traditionally, during a total war, the civilian authorities gave military commanders in the field greater authority to formulate military policies to enhance operational freedom. [Prussian military theorist Carl von] Clausewitz stated what every military man should be well aware:

> Wars are in reality . . . only the expression or manifestations of policy itself. The subordination of the political point of view to the military would be contrary to common sense, for policy has declared the War; it is the intelligent faculty, War only the instrument, and not the reverse. The subordination of the military point of view to the political is, therefore, the only thing which is possible.

Disobeying orders, thwarting diplomatic efforts, and generally frustrating the effective execution of Presidential policy all equaled insubordination.

MacArthur's View and the Failure to Comply

MacArthur tried to influence the policies of his government by "force" in misinterpreting and violating specific directives from his superiors. Truman's order issued 26 June 1950 to refrain from attacking North Korean positions beyond the 38th parallel was broadly interpreted by MacArthur and perceived as not a direct prohibition to move beyond the 38th. To him, the field commander should have the authority to ascertain the immediate combat situation and respond accordingly, despite the political repercussions. In MacArthur's mind, Truman and his Washington entourage clearly did not understand the situation on the battlefield. But in a limited war situation when politics are dominant, civilian control must be maintained to insure that only those goals are attained. Had MacArthur been allowed to pursue his own policies, the war would have been enlarged to involve Communist China, Nationalist China, and most likely, the Soviet Union, and undoubtedly would have caused some allies to withdraw their support. The allies, especially Great Britain and France, were already worried that Truman might not be able to control MacArthur. MacArthur's continued publicly voicing opposition to Administration policy, disobeying orders, thwarting diplomatic efforts, and generally frustrating the effective execution of Presidential policy all equaled insubordination to Truman as the Commander-in-Chief. He thought that his authority as President was being undermined by MacArthur and therefore, damaging his effectiveness and credibility in conducting foreign policy. As the Joint Hearings of the Senate Armed Services and Foreign Relations Committees investigated MacArthur's dismissal, most members' conclusions had finally concurred with Truman; many thought that MacArthur should have been dismissed even sooner. The President clearly had the constitutional prerogative to dismiss a military commander when deemed necessary.

Risks and Consequences

However, Truman was not unaware of the great risks involved in firing MacArthur. This awareness of risks delayed his final decision to the detriment of his credibility at home and abroad. But these are decisions, risks and consequences that must be borne by that person holding the office. In this case the consequences were loss of prestige for the office of the President and possibly World War III. However, when the military situation outruns the political objectives, the military situation must be realigned with the political considerations. In firing MacArthur on 10 April 1951, Truman began the long haul in trying to get the military situation back on track with his foreign policy and reinstate his credibility with U.S. Allies.

Problems Are Inherent in the Korean Armistice

Economist

In this 1953 article, the British magazine the *Economist* contends that the signing of the Korean War armistice will make it more urgent than ever to solve the problems of Korea. The calm acceptance by South Koreans of Communist representatives at their ports is unlikely, and dealing successfully with Communist officials and South Korean politicians will require infinite patience and tact. Additionally, so long as South Korean president Syngman Rhee and his assistants continue to reject the entire armistice project, the Allies will be hard-pressed to guarantee that South Korea will not end up violating the armistice. Other broader issues relative to the Far East, such as what to do about Communist China's claim to a seat in the United Nations, have to be addressed as well.

I s this, then, the way the war ends—with neither a bang nor a whimper, but to an accompaniment of sighs of relief mingling with discords in the West,

SOURCE. "Armistice?" *Economist,* June 13, 1953. Copyright © The Economist. Reproduced by permission.

> **Aspects of the armistice arragements bristle with potential frictions.**

defiant cries from Seoul, and seductive airs wafted from Moscow? If the firing that has now lasted for nearly three years ceases and the casualty lists come to a full stop, there will be sincere thankfulness in every heart throughout the sixteen countries that have helped to resist the aggressors in Korea. But this thankfulness must not obscure the grave problems that remain to be solved—problems which, indeed, will become more unavoidable and more urgent the instant the armistice is signed.

A Major Priority: The Problems of Korea Itself

There are, first, the problems of Korea itself. Even if the complex machinery for disposal of prisoners of war can be operated without new difficulties appearing, other aspects of the armistice arrangements bristle with potential frictions. The presence, for example, of Communist representatives at ports in South Korea will not be accepted very calmly either by the local authorities or by the population. All such difficulties could be ironed out, given goodwill; but the armistice is not being concluded in an atmosphere of goodwill. The United Nations Command and the Indian, Swiss and Swedish truce teams will need to draw on all their reserves of patience, tact and self-control if they are to treat successfully with Communist officials, alternately sullen and sly, and with South Korean politicians who are likely to be, at best, consistently sullen.

The conflicting statements of [South Korean] President [Syngman] Rhee and his assistants make it impossible, as yet, to judge how far they will carry their repudiation of the whole armistice project. Their position is strong, in that the Republic of Korea's forces now outnumber those of all its allies in South Korea; it is weak,

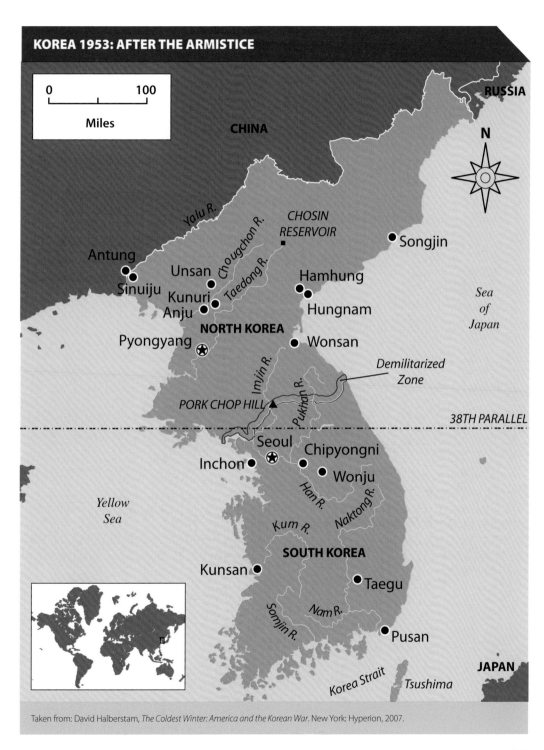

KOREA 1953: AFTER THE ARMISTICE

0 — 100
Miles

RUSSIA

CHINA

N

Yalu R.

Chougchon R.

CHOSIN RESERVOIR

Songjin

Antung

Unsan

Taedong R.

Hamhung

Sinuiju

Kunuri

Anju

Hungnam

NORTH KOREA

Pyongyang

Wonsan

Sea of Japan

Imjin R.

Demilitarized Zone

Pukhan R.

PORK CHOP HILL

38TH PARALLEL

Seoul

Chipyongni

Inchon

Wonju

Yellow Sea

Han R.

Naktong R.

Kum R.

SOUTH KOREA

Kunsan

Taegu

Somjin R.

Nam R.

Pusan

JAPAN

Korea Strait

Tsushima

Taken from: David Halberstam, *The Coldest Winter: America and the Korean War.* New York: Hyperion, 2007.

The repatriation of prisoners of war marked the truce between north and south, but there was no official end to the Korean War. (AP Images.)

in that the ROK [Republic of Korea] divisions—like the whole Korean economy—depend on American supplies, and, despite their personal loyalty to their ageing president, it is very doubtful whether in the last resort they would undertake to "go it alone." But if Mr Rhee continues to sulk in his tent, how can the allies guarantee that South Korean troops will not at some stage violate the armistice? If they cannot give such a guarantee, the Communists will have a new pretext for recalcitrance, and the "neutrals" will hesitate to get involved. But it would be both politically and militarily impossible for the allies to disarm or neutralise the ROK army, which now holds over half of the line; and even to apply economic pressure to South Korea, which the United Nations [UN] are solemnly pledged to aid in its task of reconstruction, would be a most invidious business.

An Issue to Be Resolved: Division or Reunification

Nor is this all. Even if the Seoul government and its army are induced to accept the continued division of their country, on what basis will that division rest? Theoretically, the armistice should produce a return to the situation in 1948–50, when the UN had proclaimed a united Korea as its ultimate objective, but relied on purely peaceful processes to bring it about. But in those days the tension was heightened by the fact that each of the two rival governments claimed jurisdiction over the whole of Korea, and each was recognised as the government of Korea by certain other nations, which refused recognition to its rival. Is this dangerous relationship to be re-established? It is abundantly clear that any early reunion of Korea can be achieved only by war, and the risks of war will surely be lessened if it is agreed to reduce the gap between theory and reality.

The Chinese Seat in the United Nations

This principle may, indeed, prove useful when the time comes to turn to the wider issues that remain to be settled in the Far East. Immediately after a Korean armistice, it can be taken for granted that Peking [China] will redouble its claims to the Chinese seat at Uno [United Nations Organization]; and in doing so, it will not merely be pressing for an obvious objective, but also seeking to open up a rift between the allies. But, although allied disagreement on this issue is real, and the need for agreement urgent, no good is done by exaggerating the scale of the rift or of its significance. In both Britain and America, at present, there is a tendency to assume that the other country's position as regards the Chinese seat is more absolute than is the fact; it is all too often argued that the gap is unbridgeable. In fact, since the recognition by Uno of Peking's credentials in place of those of the Taipeh government [of the Republic of China on Taiwan] would be a procedural act, the matter is largely one of simple mathematics. If and when a majority of the sixty member nations come to feel that [Chinese Communist leader] Mao [Zedong] has lived down his crime of aggression in Korea, he will receive his seat; and although groups of member nations are free to agree among themselves how and when they will vote on this issue, no one power or group of great powers could prevent the change being made if the due majority were found in favour.

The Communist China Dilemma

No one loyal to the ideal of collective security can be happy at the prospect of an unrepentant aggressor being ushered to a seat at Uno after defying that very body. Yet it should be pointed out that, far from "shooting its way into the UN," Communist China effectively delayed its appearance there by invading Korea. It has failed to buy its way in at the price of a Korean cease-fire; its application will now be considered on its merits, not under duress. More important, in reality, is the other half of the Chinese problem—the question of Formosa [Taiwan]. It is sometimes argued that the Peking Government, once seated at Uno, could demand not merely a free hand, but international support, in dealing with Formosa. But if the UN is to recognise reality by seating Peking and by tolerating Pyongyang [North Korea], is it unreasonable to ask Peking in turn to accept Formosa as a fact? As things stand, Formosa can no more be reunited with mainland China without war than can North Korea with South Korea. Why should not the side that began the war now make some concession in the cause of peace?

Other demands, too, might well be made on Peking before it is received into the international society which it has injured. But it is doubtful whether the most obvious of these—a demand for some re-assurance to China's southern neigh-bours—is worth making. Peking, like Moscow, disclaims all responsibility for Communist violence in Indo-China and Malaya, and its machina-tions in those areas cannot be ex-posed as easily as an attack across the Formosa Strait or the 38th parallel [the boundary between North and South Korea]. The security of South-East Asia must continue to rest not on promises but on what resistance can be provided there to Communist pressures. Yet, while it is to be feared that an armistice may now free Peking's hands for new adventures in the south, it is certain that failure to check aggression in Korea would have led many of the southern peoples to accept the coming of Communist rule as inevitable. In effect, the Korean campaign itself has been at more ser-vice to South-East Asia than any new negotiation can be.

> The Korean war, unlike its greater predecessors, is ending without final victory.

The True Meaning of the Korean War

Here, indeed, one arrives at the true meaning of the Ko-rean war. In fighting it, the United States and its allies have kept alight the faith in collective security that was so often allowed to die in the days of the League of Nations. In the 1930s, Abyssinia, Austria, Czechoslovakia and China itself were left alone at the mercy of the aggressor; in 1950, South Korea was not. History may record this as a unique turning point. It is true that the Korean war will leave behind it a sorry mess of unsolved problems and unaverted dangers. Let it be remembered, however, that this was true in 1918 and 1945, too. . . .

Yet there is a difference of great meaning. The Korean war, unlike its greater predecessors, is ending without final victory, with the original aggressor cowering under the skirts of his backers but spitting unrepentantly from that refuge. The nations that have given their blood in the struggle are robbed of the emotional satisfaction of triumph; small wonder that their prevailing mood is one of frustration, doubt and anger. But would it, in fact, be better if the atmosphere now reflected the jubilant relaxation, the deceptive finality, of 1918 and 1945?

This time at least, it is painfully clear that although the war may have been fought, it has not yet been won. By relaxing their vigilance, by failing to counter the political offensives which the Communists will now launch, and above all by failing to keep the ranks closed, the allies may yet yield up in peace the victory they denied the enemy in war. Their differences of opinion on the issues that now arise, and especially as regards the international status of the Peking government, are well known and well aired. The present need is to find an accommodation between them.

The Chinese Claim Victory in Korea

David Halberstam

In the following viewpoint, an American journalist asserts that the Chinese take great pride in their involvement in the Korean War. They consider Korea their victory more than anyone else's; in their view they saved the North Koreans. For China's leader, Mao Zedong, Korea was a personal victory. Mao had understood what had been at stake in Korea, had pushed to make a stand there, and had been willing to pay the cost in human life to prove that an Asian nation could hold its own against superior Western technology. Prior to his death in 2007, David Halberstam was a distinguished journalist and historian, a Pulitzer Prize winner for reporting, and the author of fifteen best sellers.

For many Americans, except perhaps a high percentage of those who had actually fought there, Korea became something of a black hole in terms of history. In the year following the cease-fire, it became

---

SOURCE. David Halberstam, *The Coldest Winter: America and the Korean War*. Hyperion Books, 2007. Copyright © 2007 Hyperion Books. All rights reserved. Reproduced by permission.

Turning the Tide of the Korean War

The CCF's [Chinese Communist Forces] entry into the war turned the tide of the war into a new phase: the war situation was transferred from offensive to defensive. The friendly forces were forced to withdraw when they were close to the Yalu and the Tumen Rivers. The war situation developed into a confrontation between the NK [North Korean] Army and the CCF vs the ROK [Republic of Korea] and UN [United Nations] forces, in other words, a showdown between Communist forces and United Nations forces. Thus the Korean War was linked with the then Cold War competition. It was the sharpest confrontation between the western and the eastern camps since the Second World War and stood at a crossroad as to whether the war would be limited to the Korean Peninsula or enlarged into another world war.

In short, China's entry into the war not only nullified the hope of unification, the nation's long cherished dream, but also forced the nation deep into the calamity of a greater war. (Consequently, though in territory the war was restricted to the Korean Peninsula, with the CCF intervention, the war at its final stage turned into a war of international character and was prolonged for two years and nine months more before it came to a cease-fire.)

SOURCE. *Korea Institute of Military History,* The Korean War, *Volume II. Lincoln, NE: The University of Nebraska Press, 2001, p. 3.*

a war they wanted to know less rather than more about. In China the reverse was true. For the Chinese it was a proud and successful undertaking, a rich part of an old nation's new history. To them it represented not just a victory, but more important, a kind of emancipation for the new China from the old China, which had so long been subjugated by powerful Western nations. The new China had barely been born, and yet it had stalemated not merely America, the most powerful nation in the world, the recent conquerors of both Japan and Germany, but the entire UN [United Nations] as well, or by their more ideological scorekeeping, all the imperialist nations of the world and their lackeys and running dogs. In that sense it had been a victory of almost immeasurable proportions, and it had been, in their minds, theirs and theirs virtually alone. The Russians had committed some hardware, but had held back at the critical moment on manpower, men who had talked big and then had cheered from the sidelines. The North Koreans had been boastful, far too confident of their own abilities, and then had failed miserably at crucial moments, and it was the Chinese who had saved them. It was not out of character and hardly a surprise in the eyes of the Chinese that the North Koreans, in their historic accounts of the war, largely withheld credit from the Chinese. They were not, the feeling went, very good about being saved. If the Chinese at that moment had lacked the military hardware to chase the Americans off Taiwan, then they had instead used their abundant manpower, their ingenuity, and the courage of their ordinary soldiers to stalemate the Westerners on land. Afterward, the rest of the world had been forced to treat China as a rising world power.

> What had been at stake in the Korean War, and it was to hang over subsequent wars in Asia, was the ability to bear a cost in human life.

Mao Zedong's Push to Take a Stand

More than that of anyone else it was [Chinese Communist leader Mao Zedong's] personal victory. He had pushed to go ahead when almost everyone else had wavered and had feared that their brand-new China, already financially and militarily exhausted by the sheer struggle of taking power after the civil war, might fail. Mao was the one who had seen the political benefits, both international and domestic, of making a stand in Korea. If the consequences had turned out to be far bloodier than

> Because the Chinese viewed Korea as a great success, Mao became more than ever the dominant figure in Chinese politics.

he had imagined, if the Americans with their superior weaponry had eventually fought better than he had expected and inflicted greater damage on his armies, then he could accept that; he had a tolerance for gore as part of the price of revolution, and he headed a nation that might not be rich in material things, but was very rich in manpower, in the numbers of men it could sacrifice on the battlefield on its way to greatness. That was something he had always believed in when most of the others around him hesitated. It was not that he knew the demographics better than the others in the leadership group; it was that he was willing to make the calculations more cold-bloodedly than they did.

An Asian Advantage

What had been at stake in the Korean War, and it was to hang over subsequent wars in Asia, was the ability to bear a cost in human life, the ability of an Asian nation to match the technological superiority of the West with the ability to pay the cost in manpower. During Korea and soon enough in Vietnam, American military commanders and theorists alike would talk about the fact that life in Asia was cheaper than it was in the West, and they would see their job as one in which they used vastly superior military technology to attain a more favorable battlefield balance, even as their Asian adversaries were determined to prove to them that in the end that was not doable, that there would always be a price and it would always be too high for an American undertaking so distant, and so geopolitically peripheral.

The Unequaled Greatness of Mao

Because the Chinese viewed Korea as a great success, Mao became more than ever the dominant figure in

Photo on following page: China's success in the Korean War made Mao loom larger in that nation's collective consciousness than did any of his fellow leaders. (Bruno Morandi/The Image Bank/Getty Images.)

Chinese politics. He had shrewdly understood the domestic political benefits of having his country at war with the Americans. As he had predicted, the war had been a defining moment between the old China and the new one, and it had helped isolate those supporters of the old China—those Chinese who had been connected to Westerners and turned them into enemies of the state. Many were destroyed—either murdered or ruined economically—in the purges that accompanied and then followed the war. From then on there was no alternative political force to check Mao; he had been the great, all-powerful Mao before the war began, and now, more than ever, his greatness was assured in the eyes of his peers on the Central Committee, who were no longer, of course, his peers. Before the war he had been the dominant figure of the Central Committee [the highest authority within the Chinese Communist Party], a man without equals; afterward he was the equivalent of a new kind of Chinese leader, a people's emperor. He stood alone. No one had more houses, more privileges, more young women thrown at him, eager to pay him homage, more people to taste his food lest he be poisoned at one of his different residences. No one could have been contradicted less frequently. The cult of personality, which he had once been so critical of, soon came to please him, and in China his cult matched that of [Soviet leader Joseph] Stalin.

The Korean War Changed the International Status Quo

William W. Stueck

In the following viewpoint taken from his 1995 chronicle of the Korean War, an expert in US diplomatic history makes the argument that the war had a great impact on the international balance of power and on other nations besides Korea. China came to be regarded as a power to be reckoned with. It also strengthened its relationship with the Soviet Union, increasing the Soviet influence on Chinese policy. China's relationship with the United States also changed, becoming more strained and combative. The war also led to a greater US military presence in Japan and, thanks to American spending there, a spike in the Japanese economy. William Stueck is a professor at the University of Georgia and the author of several books, including *Rethinking the Korean War: A New Diplomatic and Strategic History*.

SOURCE. William W. Stueck, *The Korean War.* © 1995 Princeton University Press. Reprinted by permission of Princeton University Press.

It would be inadequate to end by arguing simply that the Korean War generated a modicum of international stability in the wake of dangerous conflict, represented a victory of sorts for the United States, a defeat for the Soviet Union, and that its most tragic dimensions resulted from its prolongation through miscalculation on both sides. Those conclusions alone would assure the conflict a central place in the history of the cold war, but they would ignore numerous other dimensions of Korea's impact. . . .

The Impact of War on Korea

Perhaps the safest assertion possible in a complex and controversial subject is that the Koreans themselves were the losers, at least for the short term. While for the rest of the world the war was a limited one, both geographically and in weapons employed, for Koreans it was, as scholar Chae-Jin Lee remarks, "a 'total war' in . . . its savage destructiveness and wide-ranging consequences." . . .

Korea's losses in the number of people killed, wounded, and missing approached three million, a tenth of the entire population. Another ten million Koreans saw their families divided; five million became refugees. . . . Adding to the tragedy was the fact that the country remained divided, with little prospect for change in the foreseeable future. . . .

The most positive light that can be put on the war from the Koreans' perspective is that, once over, it was unlikely to resume. The peninsula was now an armed camp, the world in miniature, but never again would the United States let down its guard there as it had in the year before June 1950. . . .

> No one in the West ever again would dismiss China's power as General MacArthur had in the fall of 1950.

China on the Rise

If U.S. containment emerged victorious in Korea, America's failure to liberate the North reflected the reemergence of China as a great power in East Asia. In one sense, the Sino [Chinese]-U.S. clash in the war was a stalemate: neither side drove the other from the peninsula. The fighting ended near where it had begun in June 1950. Indeed, China accepted a line the balance of which was north of the 38th parallel, and it ultimately gave way to the United States on the issue of POWs [prisoners of war]. . . . Yet the end result represented a marked improvement for the Communists over the battlefield situation of October 1950, when Chinese troops entered the fray. . . . China had forced the strongest nation on earth to compromise in Korea and to accept representatives of the PRC [People's Republic of China] as equals at the bargaining table. . . . No one in the West ever again would dismiss China's power as General [Douglas] McArthur had in the fall of 1950. . . .

Clearly the war had propelled China to a position of influence in North Korea on a par with that of the Soviet Union. . . .

Whatever the perceptions of Third-World neutrals, the Korean War significantly elevated China's stature with the Soviet Union. Before China's entry into the fighting, [Joseph] Stalin had regarded the new regime as potentially akin to that in Yugoslavia. After [Chinese Communist leader] Mao [Zedong] decided to intervene in Korea, the Soviet dictator's attitude had become more respectful and supportive. Stalin's successors, lacking his prestige, became even more solicitous of China's needs. . . .

Yet increased Soviet beneficence also meant increased Soviet influence. Before the Korean War Mao had emphasized a "New Democracy-united front approach" to the recovery and development of China's economy. . . . Despite the ongoing preparations to seize Taiwan, Mao placed demobilization of his armed forces ahead of their modernization. War in Korea changed all this. The controversial nature of Mao's decision to intervene, combined with the magnified danger from abroad, led him to take drastic measures to mobilize the country. The urban bourgeoisie and the wealthy peasants became objects of harsh recrimination. Economic policy turned from recovery and balanced development through a united front with capitalists to rapid nationalization along Stalinist lines. Chinese intellectuals were pushed to the background, as Soviet advisers and party cadres dominated economic planning. Soviet models of economic development were thrust to the forefront as never before. . . .

China and Taiwan

Mao's initial choice of an alliance with the Soviets had grown out of his fear of U.S. intentions, and, in an immediate sense, the Korean War exacerbated that fear, thus increasing Chinese dependence. In the war's aftermath, PRC leaders continued to fear U.S. intentions, and they continued to use the Soviet connection for the purpose of deterrence and the advancement of internal economic development, which was critical to the modernization of their armed forces. . . .

Mao could not return to conditions of the prewar world, nonetheless, and nowhere was this more apparent than in regard to Taiwan and the offshore islands. On the eve of war, the United States showed no interest in the latter and refused to commit itself to defend the former. When the war began, the United States quickly jumped in to protect Taiwan from Communist attack. When the PRC intervened in Korea, virtually all prospects disappeared that this new U.S. policy would change for the foreseeable future. In the aftermath of war, the PRC probed [Chinese] Nationalist positions on the offshore islands of Jinmen and Matsu only to spark threats from Washington of nuclear retaliation and a formal U.S. commitment to the Nationalists to defend Taiwan. The

Soviets proved of little help through this crisis. If the final unification of China was far from inevitable in June 1950, the country's indefinite division had become reality by July 1953. . . . Even if we ignore the PRC's inability to eject UN [United Nations] forces from Korea, the new China's struggle on the peninsula had a bittersweet quality.

> Korea created or deepened certain patterns in U.S. policy toward the Third World that would come back to haunt the United States in the future.

The United States' Approach to Third World Nationalism

The same can be said of the U.S. victory. On the one hand, that victory extended well beyond Korea itself, as the demonstration of a willingness and an ability to combat "aggression" combined with the military buildup at home and in western Europe to deter such action elsewhere. For the long term, the strains placed on the Sino-Soviet alliance could not help but benefit the United States. In its competition with the Soviet Union, the United States certainly emerged the overall winner. On the other hand, Korea created or deepened certain patterns in U.S. policy toward the Third World that would come back to haunt the United States in the future. Broadly speaking, the problem may be identified as the U.S. response to Third-World nationalism. Washington never developed an effective approach to this phenomenon. . . . By pushing to the forefront in U.S. planning the military aspects of containment and the threat posed by China, the Korean War further diminished prospects for a flexible approach to the Third World that could exploit rather than confront the nationalist tide. . . .

U.S. relations with China, of course, were affected even more dramatically. . . .

The outbreak of war in Korea . . . produced a snowball effect: within five months it had led to a direct

Japan's manufacture of materiel for the Korean War effort helped make that island nation an economic power-house. (**Hulton Archive/ Getty Images.**)

Sino-U.S. confrontation on the peninsula, U.S. intervention to prevent a PRC assault on Taiwan, and deeper U.S. involvement on the French side in Indochina. In all three areas the United States seemed culpable in the eyes of most Third-World nationalists. In the first two, even America's closest allies regarded the U.S. course as ill-advised. Yet in part because of outrage with and fear of China, in part because of domestic opinion, the [President Harry] Truman administration clung to an unbending policy toward the PRC, compromising with allies and Third-World neutrals only on the scope of the war in Korea. During the remainder of the war, a struggle occurred at the United Nations between the United States and most other members over how much pressure to apply on China.

The signing of an armistice in July 1953 did little to soften the U.S. position. . . . A widespread view in the United States, especially in the Republican party, was that China policy needed tightening, not softening. . . . In accepting less than total victory in Korea, [President Dwight D. Eisenhower] used up a good deal of political capital with powerful Republicans in Congress. When the war ended, Eisenhower continued the policy of attempting to isolate Beijing from the non-Communist world. At the United Nations the United States persisted in its view that the PRC be denied admission to the international body and that the economic embargo, which was tougher on China than on the Soviet Union, be maintained. . . .

Still, the implications of the Korean War for U.S. standing in the Third World is far from one-sided. The saving of South Korea and Taiwan from communism made the United States few friends in the region. . . .

The Effect of the War on Japan

The Korean War provided an important jump start to that nation's economy. . . . During 1949 the Americans had imposed a severe austerity program, which produced a large budget surplus but also fueled unemployment and business failures. Then came the Korean War, during which Japan's gross national product grew at an annual rate of more than 10 percent. Japan's index of industrial production jumped 50 percent. . . . The source of the boom is clear. Over a four-year period beginning in June 1950, the United States spent almost three billion dollars in Japan on military-related goods and services.

Although the North Korean attack and eventual Chinese intervention increased Japanese concerns about security, the war led to an augmented U.S. military presence in the country and in the region in general. The United States also pressed Japan to rearm. Within two weeks of the outbreak of war, General MacArthur called on Japan to create a 75,000-man national police reserve and to expand by 8,000 men its maritime safety force. Japanese leaders did not realize for some time that the occupation commander intended these moves as the foundation for an army and navy, and they later resisted pressure from Washington to build up their armed forces on a large scale. The successful U.S. defense of South Korea and the American military presence in the area made this stance possible, thus enabling Japan to pursue its economic development relatively unburdened by the commitment of resources to its armed forces. . . .

The UN as an Agency of Collective Security

Given the . . . role of the United Nations in the diplomacy of the Korean War, it is appropriate to conclude with an assessment of the conflict's impact on that organization. The most obvious point is that the war did not turn the international body into an effective agency of collective security. . . . The early UN response to the invasion of South Korea produced some hope in non-Communist nations that the international body might become a critical instrument of collective action. Yet by 1953 the largely ineffective efforts of the Collective Measures Committee and the Soviet return to the Security Council called into question the ability of the United Nations to repeat its achievement in Korea. Indeed, the conflict was the lone case in the entire cold war in which the United Nations acted in an official capacity to defend a state under military attack. . . . The United States dominated the Korean enterprise, but it was unable to build on the venture to provide the United Nations with the where-withal to protect other states in the future. The trials and tribulations of U.S. diplomacy in the UN General Assembly from late 1950 to the end of the war discouraged such an effort. . . .

Nor did the United Nations emerge from Korea with an enhanced reputation for resolving international disputes. The war failed to end Korea's

> "The war, in short, did not leave the United Nations with a measurably enhanced reputation."

division, and it was instrumental in barring from membership in the United Nations the government in control of the world's most populous nation. With the PRC and the DPRK [Democratic People's Republic of Korea], not to mention the ROK, standing outside the organization, it hardly could expect to play a key role in future negotiations regarding the peninsula. Even the UN's part at crucial moments in containing the conflict in Korea by restraining the United States was not widely appreciated at the time. The war, in short, did not leave the United Nations with a measurably enhanced reputation.

The Effect on the UN as an International Organization

Yet, arguably, its response in Korea saved the United Nations from virtual extinction as a broadly inclusive international organization. On the eve of that conflict, the Soviet Union absented itself from the Security Council allegedly in protest of the Council's failure to grant the new regime in Beijing its rightful occupation of China's seat. Had the North Koreans not launched their attack in late June 1950, that particular issue would have been resolved in a matter of months in the PRC's favor, thus eliminating the Soviet excuse for its boycott. On the other hand, had the United States failed to take the lead in the United Nations in repulsing the North Korean attack, it still would have hardened its previously flexible policy on China's seat. With the PRC frozen out of the United Nations indefinitely . . . and the organization showing no sign of taking effective action on pivotal issues, Moscow would have had little reason not to withdraw completely and establish an international body of its own. If Soviet bloc countries withdrew from the United Nations, some neutrals probably would have done the same simply to avoid being associated with an organization that lacked representation from one of the two sides in the cold war. Had the United Nations become merely an organization of like-minded states in a sharply divided world, its prospects for remaining a significant force in international politics, or even for survival, certainly would have declined. The UN response to the North Korean attack eliminated this possibility, however, by demonstrating to the Soviets the liabilities entailed in their absence from the organization's key bodies. Paradoxically, the Korean War ensured the Soviet Union's ongoing membership in the United Nations at the same time that it froze out the PRC for an entire generation. . . .

> Korea was a conflict fraught with paradox.

A Conflict Full of Contradictions

Thus Korea was a conflict fraught with paradox. It pushed China and the Soviet Union closer together in an immediate sense only to generate forces that afterward would split them apart more rapidly than otherwise would have been the case. It accentuated bipolarity by increasing tensions between the superpowers and making their allies more dependent on them, but also added to the determination of many Third-World neutrals to avoid committing to either side. Although its early stages saw the United States using the United Nations effectively as an instrument of national policy, China's intervention led to others using the organization successfully in the quest to restrain the Americans. That young organization played a critical role in the conflict, but was not really strengthened as a result. China emerged from the war an overall winner, but so too did its arch enemy the United States. Perhaps the greatest paradox of all was that the conflict wrought terrible devastation to Korea, militarized the cold war as never before, and often threatened to escalate out of control, yet at its end the great powers were less likely to become directly embroiled on the battlefield than before it began. Whatever the problems it left unresolved, the war was a defining event in "the long peace" between the Soviet Union and the United States that marked the era following the holocausts of the two world wars.

The Korean War Had Far-Reaching Consequences for US Political Culture

Paul G. Pierpaoli, Jr.

In this 2001 article, Paul G. Pierpaoli, Jr., argues that the Korean War was a watershed event that had a major impact on US foreign and domestic policy, governance, and national security. The war also marked a striking change in the nation's fiscal philosophy and gave rise to three separate challenges to US constitutional governance and procedures—a presidential decision to conduct a large-scale war without a mandate from Congress, the 1951 Truman-MacArthur controversy, and a presidential order to take control of US steel mills to avoid a strike. Pierpaoli is a specialist in the Korean War and author of *Truman and Korea: The Political Culture of the Early Cold War*.

SOURCE. Paul G. Pierpaoli, Jr., "Beyond Collective Amnesia: A Korean War Retrospective," *The International Social Science Review*, 2001. Copyright © 2001 Pi Gamma Mu, Social Sciences Honor Society. Reproduced by permission.

T he Korean War was a great watershed not only for the people of the Korean Peninsula, but for the American people as well. The conflict greatly affected American foreign policy, national security policy, military policy, and domestic policy. . . .

The Militarization of American Foreign Policy

In terms of American foreign policy, the impact of the Korean War is hard to overemphasize. Between 1945 and 1950, the United States oftentimes struggled to formulate a consistent, coherent foreign policy that would keep the Soviet threat at bay, protect vital national interests, and expand liberal, free-market capitalism. And although the [President Harry] Truman administration had decided to "contain" communism even before the concept was articulated . . . , it is clear that the United States adhered to this containment mechanism—until war broke out in Korea in 1950. . . . The shock of the North Korean invasion and the American decision to intervene in Korea led to the militarization of containment and resulted in a sustained, if sometimes episodic, militarization of American foreign policy. . . . President Truman picked up the gauntlet in June of 1950 and greatly expanded America's commitment to fight perceived communist aggression. As a consequence, America's traditional ideological trilogy of anti-militarism, isolationism, and antistatism was forever banished to the history books. . . .

Change in US Foreign Policy and Defense Commitments

When Harry Truman committed American forces to battle in June 1950, he unveiled a veritable Trojan Horse for American foreign and defense policy. Only hours after he decided to draw the line in Korea, he dispatched the U.S. Seventh Fleet to the Taiwan Straits, formally committing the United States to the defense of Taiwan and [head of the Chinese Nationalist government in exile on Taiwan] Jiang Jieshi's Kuomintang government. This move no doubt greatly antagonized [Chinese Communist leader] Mao Zedong's regime on the Chinese mainland, further soured U.S.-Chinese relations—even before the intervention in Korea—and ensured a separate and semi-independent Taiwan that would prove repeatedly to be a source of contention between the United States and the PRC [People's Republic of China]. . . .

The impact of the Korean War on U.S. foreign policy was certainly not limited to the "two Chinas" [Nationalist China on Taiwan and Communist China on the mainland] and the Korean Peninsula, for the conflict led the Truman administration to reassess in total its foreign policy and defense commitments all around the world. After the outbreak of the war, the United States increased significantly its aid to France, which at the time was fighting its own war in Indochina. Fearing a regional or even a world-wide Communist insurgency, America stiffened its resolve to fight communism throughout Asia. This decision would have profound implications down the line. Slowly and steadily, beginning in 1950 and 1951, the United States committed itself to stopping the Communist insurgency in Vietnam. Thus, for the United States, the Korean War was the Alpha event that led to its eventual descent down the slippery slope of war in Indochina. The effects of the Korean War certainly did not go unnoticed in Japan, either. Japan was used as a major staging area during the conflict, and wartime spending rehabilitated the war-ravaged Japanese economy. Furthermore, the United States would now view Japan as the economic and political engine of American-style liberal capitalism in East Asia. . . . On the European continent, the Korean

> Korea forced the Truman administration to equilibrate America's foreign policy goals and commitments with its military capabilities.

War gave the Truman administration the perfect pretext for fully militarizing the nascent NATO [North Atlantic Treaty Organization]. . . .

Bipartisan Troubles at Home

The Korean War also poisoned—at least temporarily—the well of foreign policy bipartisanship. Truman's decision to send troops to Korea and more troops to Europe without Congressional approval sparked a heated debate in Congress that resulted in the so-called "Great Debate" of late 1950 and early 1951. In the end, the Truman administration won the battle . . . , but it was a Pyrrhic victory [gained at too high a cost] to be sure. As the war grew more unpopular and then stalemated, the president's foes—which were by then legion—attacked and criticized him at every turn. By mid-1951, the Korean War had indeed become "Truman's war" and he was forced to go it largely alone, navigating the desolate political wilderness of an unpopular, limited war by himself. In the end, Truman, like Lyndon Johnson a decade and a half later, became a virtual prisoner of the war he set in motion. In 1952, as in 1968, foreign policy miscalculations, misapplied military power, and an unpopular war would bring down a sitting president and repudiate his political party.

The NSC-68 and US Military Policy

The Korean War also marked a distinct turning point in American Cold War geostrategy, national security policy, and . . . military policy. The changes wrought in these areas are perhaps less dramatic than those in the foreign policy arena, but they are nonetheless critical to understanding the catalytic nature of the conflict. Clearly, Korea forced the Truman administration to equilibrate America's foreign policy goals and commitments with its military capabilities. . . . By January 1950, however, the president partially acceded to these pressures by

US soldiers in South Korea during the Vietnam War. The Korean conflict put the United States on a war footing in the region and was a precursor to Vietnam. (**AP Images.**)

authorizing the development and eventual deployment of the hydrogen bomb. But in April 1950, when he was first shown the NSC-68 [National Security Report 68, the blueprint for waging the Cold War] recommendations, he refused to authorize their implementation. . . . In the end, Truman reluctantly agreed to implement NSC-68 only AFTER the outbreak of war in Korea. . . . This sudden reversal brought on by the Korean War finally brought America's military capabilities in-line with its ever-widening and far-flung foreign policy and military commitments.

If the decision to implement NSC-68 balanced American commitments with the nation's capacity to fulfill them, it also unleashed a torrent of short-term and long-term repercussions, many of which were unforeseen and would result in permanent alterations to the political and economic scenes. The impact of the decision obviously affected U.S. military and mobilization policy. Most of the NSC-68-inspired military buildup was earmarked NOT for the war in Korea, but rather for a much broader, sustained, and vaguely indefinite Cold War buildup. What the United States was to witness beginning in the fall of 1950 was in fact a "mobilization within a mobilization." That is, the Truman administration engaged the nation in an immediate buildup in order to fight the hot war in Korea while at the same time it began to gird the nation to wage a far-flung and protracted Cold War. Thus, the massive, Korean-era military rearmament program became the nation's de facto Cold War readiness program, designed to outlast the war in Korea and to enable the nation to fight—at minimum—two regional, Korea-sized wars simultaneously with enough reserve to maintain an adequate defense of the homeland and the NATO allies. A monumental effort, to be sure, the Korean rearmament program provided for the construction of a permanent, institutionalized mobilization base to ensure that the United States would never again be forced to mobilize from scratch. . . . Building the Cold War mobilization base resulted in profound changes to the nation's political economy and political culture. . . .

Drastic Changes in the US Budget

The nearly simultaneous decision to intervene in the Korean War and to begin the implementations of NSC-

68 resulted in the quadrupling of the U.S. defense budget. . . . Such a dramatic military buildup undertaken in such a short period of time caused innumerable short-term and long-term dislocations to the economies of the United States and Western Europe. . . . Two rounds of high inflation hit the United States in rapid succession—the first one in the summer of 1950 and the second in the late fall of 1950. The second inflationary period was a direct result of the Chinese intervention in the Korean War, which forced the Truman administration to step up mobilization dramatically and led American consumers to embark on a new wave of panic buying and hoarding. Thus, by January 1951 Truman invoked mandatory wage, price, and credit controls and created a panoply of new mobilization agencies designed to carry out the exigencies of the stepped-up rearmament program and to stabilize the overheating economy. The results of these decisions were predictable: government bureaucracies grew at an alarming rate, the power of the federal government—especially the Executive branch—became more expansive, tax burdens became heavier, budget deficits ballooned, and industry and consumers alike began to bristle at the substantial increase in governmental intrusion and regulation. In short, the modern, post-World War II national security state was born during the Korean War, which was never to be largely or wholly dismantled. Massive defense spending also tightened the ties between the federal government and private enterprise as well as academia in general and the hard sciences in particular. . . .

> "The modern, post-World War II national security state was born during the Korean War."

The decision to mobilize for the long haul of the Cold War meant that balanced federal budgets in America were no longer sacrosanct. . . . What is clear is that the Korean War marked a dramatic change in the nation's fiscal ideology and policymaking. That is, instead of determining the aggregate budget and adjusting defense spending accordingly, the opposite became the norm after 1950: policy makers calculated defense needs first and then adjusted aggregate fiscal policy to meet the demands of national security. . . .

> The decision to keep the nation partially but permanently mobilized essentially created an entirely new economy within the confines of the existing one.

A New Economy

The decision to build and maintain in perpetuity a Cold War mobilization base and to keep defense spending at high levels resulted in several interesting developments. Constructing the mobilization base meant building excess industrial capacity and funding esoteric, defense-related research and development programs that could swing into immediate action at the first sign of crisis. These arrangements further increased the size and scope of the government and tightened the ties between the public and private sectors. Not only that, but the decision to keep the nation partially but permanently mobilized essentially created an entirely new economy within the confines of the existing one. This "new" economy, which some scholars and critics have dubbed the "military-industrial complex," greatly accelerated changes already in progress in the U.S. economy and industrial landscape. . . . What's more, as these new industrial and commercial areas blossomed, reduced tax revenues and the drain of educated and skilled workers—the so-called "white flight"—left the older cities of the Northeast and Midwest in a terrible quandary. They became increasingly dominated by large numbers of permanently displaced, low-tech, blue-collar workers and a growing urban underclass. And lacking the tax base and resources to properly educate and train their citizenry, many of these cities fell into perpetual hard times. The monetary costs incurred by the Korean-era rearmament effort were high indeed; higher still, it seems, were the human and intellectual costs of the trends unleashed by the Korean conflict. . . .

Three Challenges to US Constitutional Authority

The effects of the Korean War on the American political and constitutional systems are already well known and documented. They bear repeating here, however, because they too fit into the pattern of Korea as a great watershed event. The war in Korea precipitated three separate challenges to American constitutional governance and procedures. First, Harry Truman's decision to wage a large-scale war without a congressional mandate, thousands of miles away, in which millions of U.S. soldiers fought, was an unprecedented abrogation of congressional authority and prerogative. . . . The second challenge to American constitutional prescriptions revolved around the Truman-MacArthur controversy of 1951. General Douglas MacArthur's repeated attempts to circumvent presidential orders and to use the war to further his own specific political agenda resulted in the further politicization of the Korean War and called into question the supremacy of civilian control over the military. Truman dealt effectively with the crisis by firing MacArthur, but the episode conjured up the specter of America as a kind of Cold War Sparta. . . . Finally, President Truman's order to seize the nation's steel mills in 1952 to avoid a strike precipitated yet another constitutional crisis involving the issue of presidential powers and national security imperatives. The U.S. Supreme Court ruled the president's action unconstitutional, but the episode once

> The Korean conflict institutionalized an ongoing trend in twentieth-century American history: the estrangement of the government from the governed.

more raised fears of America as a Cold War garrison state and some saw the American presidency as coming perilously close to a Cold War dictatorship.

McCarthyism and the American Democratic Process

I would be remiss if I did not mention here the impact that the war had on the politics of anti-communism, especially the noxious politics of McCarthyism. Although the Truman administration itself helped to launch the era of rabid anti-communism through its pre-Korean security and loyalty programs, no American was more responsible for taking the issue to the extreme than Senator Joseph R. McCarthy (R-WI). McCarthy began his anti-communist witch-hunt and attempted purges in February 1950, some four months prior to the outbreak of war in Korea. But there should be no doubt the war fully unleashed McCarthy and gave him a perfect foil. In fact, it is almost impossible to conceive of the era we know as McCarthyism in America without the Korean War. . . . The Korean War and the McCarthyism it unleashed also sounded the death knell for the traditional American Left. . . .

Just as ominously, the Korean War-era rearmament program and the concomitant decision to implement NSC-68 had a profoundly transformative effect on the American democratic process as well. The Korean conflict institutionalized an ongoing trend in twentieth-century American history: the estrangement of the government from the governed. The process of building the Cold War national security state, which began in earnest in 1950 and 1951, resulted in a fundamentally undemocratic national security apparatus. During and after Korea, legions of unelected "experts," bureaucrats, and resurrected "dollar-a-year" men began to push aside elected leaders and other publicly appointed officials. The result was a national security and foreign policy process that became increasingly secretive and wholly unresponsive to the average citizen. Thus, decisions that affected the fundamental workings of the government and the policy making process itself became less and less informed by the will of the people, in whom the sovereignty of the U.S. government supposedly rests. More and more issues that directly affected the American citizenry were hidden from view, under the guise of national security. . . .

A Major Change of Perspective

It should now be clear that the Korean War had dramatic and far-reaching consequences, many of which are with us still, fifty years after the war began. It is to my way of thinking an "Alpha" event that significantly transformed Korean, American, and international history. Whether one chooses to view it from a more traditional, bipolar Cold War perspective or from a Korean or East Asian perspective, the Korean War changed the perspective and discourse of confrontation and hegemony in the post-World War II era.

It's Time to Bring American Troops Home from Korea

Stephen Erickson

The following viewpoint, written in 2010, contends that US troops should not be in South Korea. Keeping troops there in readiness for combat may have been necessary during the Cold War, but the Cold War ended long ago, the author says. Furthermore, South Korea is much more advanced and prosperous than North Korea and should be able to defend itself against North Korea should the need arise; South Korean and US policies often do not mesh; and not all South Koreans want American troops in their country. Given its many commitments elsewhere, he explains, the US military is stretched too thin to be able to play a major role in defending South Korea on the ground in a new Korean War. Stephen Erickson is the executive director of CenterMovement.org.

SOURCE. Stephen Erickson, "End the Cold War in Korea: Bring American Troops Home Before It's Too Late." Copyright © CenterMovement.org. Reproduced by permission.

On the night of March 26 [2010] the South Korean 1,200-ton warship Cheonan patrolled the boundary waters between North and South Korea. At 10:45 an explosion near the bow rocked the vessel and sank the Cheonan, taking the lives of 46 crew members with it. Although the investigation is still ongoing, the South Korean Defense Minister has declared that a torpedo is the likeliest source of the blast. North Korea appears to have destroyed the South Korean warship.

Normally such an unprovoked attack would start a war, but the Korean peninsula is not a normal place. The Koreans, with their strong sense of nationalism, remain divided along the 38th parallel, with a 2.5 mile "demilitarized zone" between them. Meanwhile approximately 28,000 US troops still help guard the border. An armistice formally ended hostilities in Korea in 1953, but officially the war never ended. No peace treaty was ever signed. One year ago, the North formally and ominously withdrew from the armistice.

North Korea vs. South Korea

North Korea, a tiny country with the world's 4th largest standing army, is the most militarized society in the world. It has a standing army of 1.2 million soldiers, and a peasant militia with as many as 4 million reserves. Some 13,000 artillery pieces, dug into the hills within range of the South Korean capital of Seoul, are poised to obliterate the South's most important city upon "The Dear Leader's" command. Some estimates suggest that as many as one million South Koreans could die under such an assault. Then there's the matter of North Korea's several nuclear weapons.

South Korea, officially the "Republic of Korea," has about half as many soldiers as the North, but they are better trained and far better equipped. South Korea is wealthy and technologically advanced. North Korea has half the population and 1/30th the economy of the

The Korean DMZ

With the idea of dividing Korea into spheres of influence in 1896, Japan and Russia conducted negotiations that almost resulted in the partition of Korea along a mid-peninsula boundary line, though not at the thirty-eighth parallel, where the Demilitarized Zone (DMZ) is now nominally situated. That division was not to take place for more than fifty years, and then as a consequence of World War II and the Korean War. Thus, the DMZ became a symbol of the US's Cold War containment policy. Now it is a stark remnant of that standoff. . . .

Since the end of the Korean War in 1953, the DMZ has been essentially off limits to all but a few residents living in two showcase villages, one in North Korea and one in South Korea. . . . It has been part of a geopolitical vacuum and memory of war. It and the Civilian Control Zone (CCZ) on the south side also have been home to at least one million land mines, reinforcing the DMZ's barbed wire perimeter extending along much of its length. . . . The natural and cultural resources contained in the DMZ and CCZ represent millions of years of evolution, some of its species being found nowhere else in the world, and thousands of years of human history, at least 5,000 of which have been home to a people identified as distinctly Korean.

SOURCE: *Hall Healy, "Korean Demilitarized Zone: Peace and Nature Park," International Journal on World Peace, Vol. XXIV, No. 4 (December 2007), pp. 61–62.*

South. While the rulers of the North live lavishly, famine killed a million people in the 1990s, and the United Nation's World Food Program is worried that this year [2010] may witness the worst food shortages since then.

Soldiers march at a US base in Seoul. Many argue that South Korea is quite capable of defending itself from its northern neighbor and that US troops are no longer needed to aid in combat readiness. (Jung Yeon-Je/ AFP/Getty Images.)

Starving people can be dangerous people. Historically North Korea uses its military, its only strength, as leverage to obtain outside assistance.

South Korea today might well be able to ultimately defend itself against the North, but the bloodshed would be horrific. A key factor in any future conflict is Seoul's location so near the North. Experts suggest that a recently revised North Korean military strategy consists of swiftly taking Seoul and holding the city's millions of people as hostages.

All of this begs a couple of important questions. How many more South Korean ships can be torpedoed before the South retaliates, surely starting a larger war? And, what are 28,000 American troops doing in the middle of this Korean powder keg?

> The permanent US military deployment in South Korea is a Cold War anachronism.

As the sinking of the Cheonan clearly indicates, the sparks are already flying.

An Unnecessary and Unwanted Presence

The permanent US military deployment in South Korea is a Cold War anachronism. There is absolutely no reason that a nation as advanced and prosperous as South Korea cannot defend itself from its pathetically backward northern brothers and sisters. A well-known night-time satellite image taken from space shows a brilliant South and a North languishing in the Dark Ages.

The US presence creates political dysfunction while it minimally protects South Korea. US soldiers on South Korean soil breed resentment. Thousands of nationalist South Korean students regularly take to the streets to protest the Americans soldiers in their country and to call for unification between North and South.

Out-of-Step Policies and Future Possibilities

South Korean and US government policies are often awkwardly out of step with each other, with America often having the far more hawkish posture as it did during the [President George] W. Bush years. American security guarantees have perhaps sometimes led the government of the South to engage in policies of inappropriate appeasement toward the North.

The threat of South Korea investing in nuclear weapons to counter the North might, for example, finally persuade China to put sufficient pressure on North Korea. A South Korea determined to match North Korean nuclear weapons development might paradoxically further the goal of a nuclear-free Korean peninsula.

Most crucially, from an American point of view, the US Army is stretched too thin to play much of a role in protecting South Korea. As things stand, American soldiers are little more than targets for North Korean artillery and missiles. A defense of Seoul, its re-conquest, and forcible regime change in the North are all beyond US military capabilities at this time, given its commitments elsewhere. US participation on the ground in a new Korean War would also stress the US federal budget beyond the breaking point.

The United States never properly created a new foreign and defense policy when the Cold War ended. Instead, it has generally maintained its Cold War military posture, with bases and commitments strewn throughout the globe, even as new challenges since 9/11 have called American forces to new missions. The US military presence in Korea is a Cold War artifact that needs to be brought home before it's too late.

American Troops Play an Essential Role in Korea

Walter L. Sharp

In a speech given before the Senate Armed Services Committee in 2009, the top US general in Korea maintains that the alliance of the Republic of Korea and the United States, entered into more than fifty years ago, has benefited both nations. He argues that US presence in Northeast Asia, an area in which the United States has considerable national security interests, is a long-term investment in regional stability. General Walter L. Sharp is commander of the United Nations Command, commander of the Republic of Korea-United States Combined Forces, and commander of the United States Forces Korea.

A s the Commander, United Nations Command (UNC); Commander, Republic of Korea—United States (U.S.) Combined Forces Command (CFC);

SOURCE. Walter L. Sharp, statement before the Senate Armed Services Committee, March 19, 2009.

> The U.S. gained a stalwart ally and strategic partner with unwavering dedication to the defense of peace and freedom in a challenging part of the world.

and Commander, United States Forces Korea (USFK), it is a privilege to represent the Soldiers, Sailors, Airmen, Marines, Department of Defense (DoD) Civilians, and their families who serve in the Republic of Korea (ROK). . . . Your vital support allows us to ensure the security of the ROK, promote prosperity and stability in Northeast Asia, and protect our shared national interests in the region. . . .

The ROK-US Alliance: A Mutually Beneficial Partnership

For the last 56 years, since ratification of the Mutual Defense Treaty by the U.S. and the ROK, the ROK-U.S. Alliance has deterred aggression, maintained peace on the Korean Peninsula, and promoted security and stability in this vital region. Our bilateral Alliance has served both nations well. The ROK transformed from a country devastated by war to a vibrant democracy with the world's 14th largest economy. The U.S. gained a stalwart ally and strategic partner with unwavering dedication to the defense of peace and freedom in a challenging part of the world. ROK armed forces fought alongside Americans in Vietnam and participated in Operation Desert Storm. More recently, the ROK has deployed forces to Iraq and Afghanistan, being the third largest contributor of forces to Operation Iraqi Freedom during most of the 2004 to 2008 time period. The ROK's five-year presence in northern Iraq contributed significantly to the stabilization and reconstruction of that country. Similarly, the ROK currently maintains a civilian medical and vocational training team in Afghanistan and has contributed assistance to that country worth millions of dollars. On a broader scale, the ROK has also participated in United Nations (UN) peacekeeping operations, currently having a presence in six operations around the world. The ROK also deployed the Cheonghae unit—which consists of a 4,500-ton destroyer and an anti-submarine helicopter—to the waters off Somalia for the conduct of anti-piracy operations.

> In 2008, our governments agreed to maintain the current level and capability of U.S. force presence on the Korean Peninsula for the foreseeable future.

[South Korea's] President Lee Myung-bak's efforts to maintain regional security and stability include robust, economically-focused, and results-oriented regional outreach initiatives. Within the first year of his term of office, President Lee has conducted multiple summits with each of the national leaders of China, Japan, Russia, and the U.S. President. Lee and his cabinet actively participated in our Ulchi Freedom Guardian exercise in August 2008 and promised even more participation in 2009. Measures aimed at strengthening the ROK-U.S. Alliance, establishing strategic partnerships with China and Russia, and working with Japan and China on a multi-lateral response to the recent global financial crisis demonstrates his resolve to achieve a more prosperous, stable, and secure future for the ROK.

Added Strength Through New Measures

In the past year our two nations have taken significant actions to enhance the military capabilities of and reinforce the mutual trust that underscores this great Alliance. In 2008, our governments agreed to maintain the current level and capability of U.S. force presence on the Korean Peninsula for the foreseeable future. This is a clear and visible statement of U.S. commitment to the Alliance. Our two nations also concluded host nation burden sharing negotiations, resulting in a Special Measures Agreement (SMA) that will provide ROK funding support for U.S. forces in Korea over the next five years.

And I thank you for passing legislation that elevated the ROK's Foreign Military Sales (FMS) status to be on par with NATO [North Atlantic Treaty Organization] countries and other longstanding allies. This legislation will enhance interoperability with the ROK and the Alliance's warfighting capability. Finally, the U.S. DoD approved proceeding with implementation of three-year accompanied tours for service members assigned to Seoul, Pyeongtaek, Osan, Daegu and Chinhae. This constitutes a major step forward in ending our outdated system of one-year unaccompanied tours for the large majority of service members assigned to Korea. These measures will

A South Korean medic examines a patient at a US air base in Afghanistan. Ongoing US support has made South Korea a steady ally in other world conflicts. **(Musadeq Sadeq/ AP Images.)**

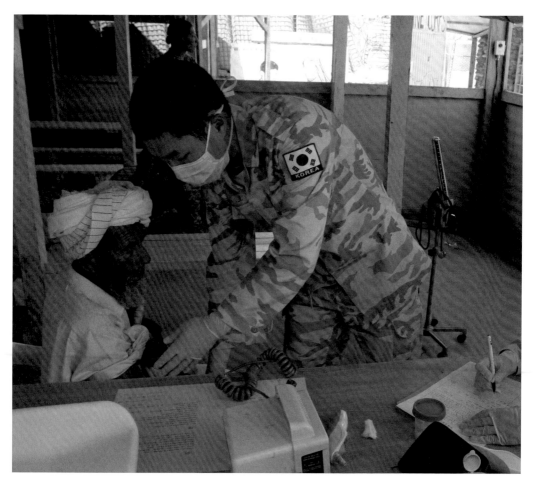

strengthen the Alliance and improve our ability to promote regional security and stability in Northeast Asia.

Strategic Importance of Northeast Asia

The U.S. has significant national security interests in Northeast Asia. With five of the world's 19 largest economies located in the region and a combined 2008 gross domestic product (GDP) of $16.6 trillion (23.5 percent of global GDP), Northeast Asia is a crucial component of the global economy. The ROK plays a vital role in a region that accounts for 22 percent of all U.S. trade in goods. It is a first-class economic power, our seventh largest trading partner and one of the most technologically and scientifically advanced countries in the world that boasts the world's largest shipbuilding industry.

While Northeast Asia generates a significant share of the world's commerce, it is also characterized by uncertainty, complexity, and rapid change, and has consistently posed difficult security challenges to the international community. Beyond the North Korean threat, the presence of four of the world's six largest militaries and two proven nuclear powers (China and Russia), not including the U.S., as well as historical animosities, territorial disputes, resource competition, and historical struggles for regional hegemony combine to pose long-term regional security challenges. The ROK sits at the nexus of a region influenced by—and influencing—an emerging China, a resurgent Russia, and a prosperous Japan.

U.S. presence in Northeast Asia is a long-term investment in regional stability with specific objectives: promoting democracy and free market economies; preserving peace and stability in the region; engaging other regional powers; and setting the conditions for denuclearization and the eventual peaceful reunification of the Korean Peninsula. A strong Alliance, with a meaningful U.S. force presence, is absolutely essential to meeting these objectives. U.S. forces in Korea are adapting to changing conditions in this dynamic region. We are transforming into more modern and capable warfighting units and headquarters, while preparing to assume a doctrinally supporting role after the transition of ROK wartime operational control (OPCON) to the Korean government on April 17, 2012. An enduring U.S. force presence in Korea after OPCON transition in 2012 will ensure a strong Alliance fully capable of meeting its treaty commitments well into the future. . . .

An Evolving and Enduring Alliance

The ROK-U.S. Alliance is one of the greatest bilateral success stories in modern history. In 1950, the UNC was created to defend the ROK when it was attacked by North Korea. In 1957, establishment of USFK provided a command structure to fully support the Alliance. In 1978, the Alliance further evolved with the creation of the CFC, a unified ROK and U.S. command structure. The Alliance evolved once again in 1994 when peacetime OPCON of ROK forces was transferred to the ROK. With the transition of wartime OPCON to the ROK in 2012, the U.S. and the ROK will enter a new era of cooperation, an era marked by a Republic of Korea with defense responsibilities commensurate with its capabilities and sovereign rights. After 2012, the ROK-U.S. Alliance needs to remain strong in order to preserve peace and stability on the Korean Peninsula as well as in the region as a whole.

> The Alliance is more relevant to the national interests of the U.S. than it has ever been.

Today the Alliance is more relevant to the national interests of the U.S. than it has ever been. It will remain essential to the protection and advancement of U.S. national interests in this strategically vital region of the world. We look forward to continuing this vital partnership, one that promotes freedom, democracy, and global free trade in Northeast Asia. Moving forward together, I am more confident than ever that this Alliance will continue to maintain peace and stability in a region for which Americans, side-by-side with our Korean partners, have shed blood.

CHAPTER 3

Personal Narratives

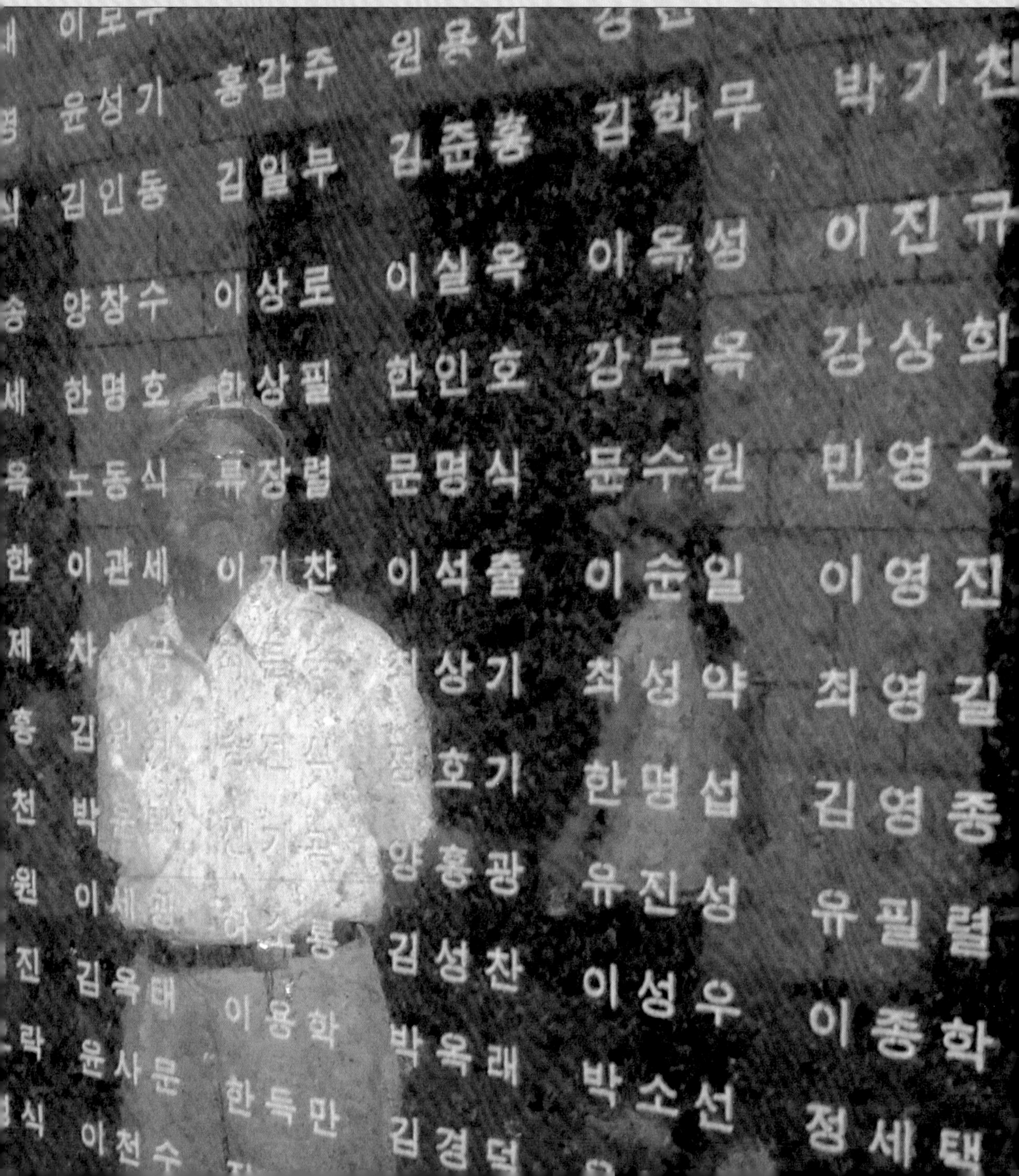

An American Journalist Reports from the Korean Battlefront

Marguerite Higgins

In the following viewpoint, written in 1951, a newspaper correspondent recounts her experiences reporting from Korea at the beginning of the war. She describes the sights, scents, and mood as she and three other correspondents headed to the battalion command post at Pyontek. She speaks of the sense of unreality she felt and describes the first US casualty of the war. She goes on to share her incredulity upon learning that the US bazooka teams had been forced to retreat after facing Soviet tanks. Marguerite Higgins was an internationally recognized American reporter and war correspondent. She broke the glass ceiling for female correspondents and was the first woman to win a Pulitzer Prize for international reporting.

Photo on previous page: A South Korean veteran reads the names of fallen soldiers on a monument in the Korean War Memorial in Seoul. The war claimed millions of lives. (**Park Ji-Hwan/ AFP/Getty Images.**) Photo on follow-

SOURCE. Marguerite Higgins, *War in Korea: The Report of a Woman Combat Correspondent*. Copyright © 1951 by Marguerite Higgins. Used by permission of Doubleday, a division of Random House, Inc.

The Korean monsoon was still in full downpour . . . when our jeepload of correspondents started to the front to watch Americans dig in—and die—in their first battle.

On the Road to Pyontek

As we left the little gray house at [the South Korean city of] Taejon's outskirts around three in the morning, our conversation was as somber as the weather. We were going to Pyontek, where only the day before our forces had been badly strafed by our own planes. This was the first of many incidents which showed how much we needed to improve our ground-air co-ordination. I was assigned now to watch the sides and give warning if I saw a plane.

> The smell of death rose from the ditches and the waterlogged rice paddies on either side of the road.

As we neared Pyontek we had to drive around blackened, still-burning ammo trucks. And by the side of the road were the mutilated bodies of scores of hapless refugees who had been caught in the strafing. The smell of death rose from the ditches and the waterlogged rice paddies on either side of the road. . . .

Sorting It Out: To Stay or To Go

Aside from the general melancholy of the morning, I had some purely personal reasons for being unhappy. There has been some publicity about a feud between me and one of my *Herald Tribune* colleagues. . . .

The simple fact was that my colleague didn't want me to stay in Korea at all. I had cabled the office at home that I very much wanted to stay, that I believed there was more than enough news to share and that the war could be covered on a partnership basis. My colleague disagreed with this to the point where he told me flatly that I would be fired if I didn't get back to Tokyo and stay there. . . .

ing page: Journalist Marguerite Higgins—seen here in the cargo hold of a plane over South Korea in 1950—witnessed fear, courage, and death during her reportage of the war. (Carl Mydans/Time & Life Pictures/Getty Images.)

A farmer leads an ox

I was in such a state of physical exhaustion that I was unusually vulnerable emotionally and really felt baffled and upset. But . . . I found some fine moral support in Korea. Carl ("Stumpy") Mydans of *Time* and *Life*, a wonderfully kind human being, had unwittingly become mixed up in my problem because my colleague had warned him that if he took me to the front I would be fired. I talked it all over with Carl, and he helped me make up my mind with this question, "What is more important to you, Maggie, the experience of covering the Korean war or fears of losing your job?" Right then I decided to go back to the front, no matter what came of it.

But there was no denying that I was heavyhearted. I felt that no matter what the cause of my colleague's hostility, it would be harder on me because I was a woman. Since I was the only woman here doing a daily newspaper job, I was bound to be the target for lots of talk, and this mix-up would supply fresh material. I believed that no matter who was right, I would undoubtedly be blamed.

But I was happily wrong. The men correspondents on the scene in Korea could not have been more fair. They did the only sensible thing, which was to refuse to take sides at all. By the end of the summer the entire situation ended up where it belonged, in the joke department.

A Call for Bazooka Teams

But at Pyontek that morning there was only gloom in the air and in my mind. We were all cold and tired by the time we found the battalion command post hidden in a tiny thatched hut surrounded by a sea of mud. Colonel Harold ("Red") Ayres, commander of the first battalion of the 84th Infantry Regiment, shared his command post with a filthy assortment of chickens, pigs, and ducks.

We had barely had time to enjoy a cup of hot coffee when Brigadier General George B. Barth strode into

138

the hut. "Enemy tanks are heading south," he said. "Get me some bazooka teams pronto."

Then, apparently aware of our startled reaction, he added, "Those Communist tanks are going to meet Americans for the first time—Colonel Smith's battalion is up forward. We can depend on him to hold on, but if any tanks do get by those batteries they'll head straight for here."

> I was filled with a very uncomfortable mixture of apprehension and excitement as we followed the bazooka teams to the unknown front.

Going into Battle

So America's raw young troops, boys who had reached the Korean front only a few hours before, were going into battle. It was a big moment, and we four knew that we had been cut in on a critical slice of history. We were about to see the beginning of what we later named the long retreat.

I was filled with a very uncomfortable mixture of apprehension and excitement as we followed the bazooka teams to the unknown front. Wrapped in rain-soaked blankets, we traveled swiftly behind the small convoy of trucks and command cars carrying the bazooka and rifle teams. Then, on the crest of a hill, the convoy suddenly halted. We could see soldiers lumping out of the trucks and spreading out on a ridge parallel to the road. The road was dogged with South Korean soldiers in what seemed an endless procession southward. (South Koreans, in these early days, simply appropriated the jeeps or command cars assigned to them and took off individually.) One South Korean soldier on horseback, his helmet camouflaged with bits of branches sticking up at absurd angles, came cantering toward us, shouting, "Tanks! Tanks! Tanks! Go back."

"Now wait a minute," said [correspondent Ray] McCartney in his quiet British tone. "Even if tanks do show, no infantry has been sighted. Tanks can't get off the road, and we can. Let's walk on."

Tanks in Sight

A little farther on we found Lieutenant Charles Payne—a dapper, fast-talking young veteran of World War II. He had been examining the marks of huge tank treads on the road and told us that the tank had sighted us, turned around, and backed into a near-by village. "We're going to dig in here," he added, "and send out patrols to hunt him down."

But the tank didn't require any hunting. Even as we were entrenching in a graveyard flanking the main road, the enormous thing rumbled into view about fifteen hundred yards to our left. It was astraddle a railroad, and there was a second tank behind it. We had no idea how many more tanks might be in the little village that lay between us and Colonel Smith's battalion. And, to make things even more tense, Colonel Smith's battalion was now urgently messaging us for ammunition. Unless the tanks were smashed, his forward battalion would be cut off.

The Wisdom of Experience

At this point a small ammunition-laden convoy roared up the road. Two lieutenants jumped out and rushed up the hill to Lieutenant Payne. They were tall, fine-looking officers with all the bravado and eagerness of very young, very green soldiers. One announced theatrically to Payne, "Charlie, our orders are to crash through with this ammunition and to hell with the sniper fire. We'll make it all right, but we'd like you to give us a couple of your men."

Somewhat owlishly, but in a voice that bespoke authority, Lieutenant Payne said, "Things are changing a bit. We'll just wait and make another check with headquarters. Then maybe we'll make like Custer."

Roy and I both smiled at that. We were becoming increasingly impressed with the sure, professional way Payne was handling the situation. I had asked him earlier in the day how he felt about being back at war.

> From our graveyard foxholes we saw the . . . first American death in Korea.

"Well," he said, "when I learned in Japan that I was coming over here I was plain scared to death—I figured that I'd run through my share of good luck in Italy. A man's only got a certain number of close calls coming to him. But as soon as I heard the guns I got over it."

Payne would really have been worried if he had known just how very hard he was going to have to press his share of good luck. When I saw him again in August, he and Colonel Ayres were the only two survivors of the battalion headquarters staff of eleven. Of the battalion itself, about 900 men at full strength, only 263 were still on the line. The rest were wounded or dead.

Bazooka Fire, a Belch of Flame, and a Death

From our graveyard foxholes we saw the first of these deaths—the first American death in Korea.

When orders to attack first went out to the fifty-odd youngsters in our bazooka team they gazed at the tanks as if they were watching a newsreel. It took prodding from their officers to make them realize that this was it— that it was up to them to attack. Slowly, small groups of them left their foxholes, creeping low through the wheat field toward the tank. The first swoosh from a bazooka flared out when they were nearly five hundred yards away from the tanks. But the aim was good and it looked like a direct hit.

But apparently it didn't look good to Lieutenant Payne. "Damn," he said, "those kids are scared—they've got to get close to the tanks to do any damage."

The first Communist tank whose turret rose above the protecting foliage along the railway answered the bazooka with a belch of flame. We could see enemy soldiers jump from the tank, and machine guns began to chatter at the approaching bazooka teams. Through my field glasses I could see a blond American head poke up out of the grass—the young soldier was trying to adjust his aim. Flashes from the tank flicked the ground horribly close, and I thought I saw him fall. It was so murky I wasn't sure. But in a few minutes I heard a soldier shout, "They got Shadrick—right in the chest. He's dead, I guess."

> It seemed incredible that we were going to pull back with enemy tanks still within our lines.

The tone of voice was very matter-of-fact. I thought then how much more matter-of-fact the actuality of war is than any of its projections in literature. The wounded seldom cry—there's no one with time and emotion to listen.

A Need to Pull Back

Bazookas were still sounding off. We felt certain that the tanks, which were like sitting ducks astride the tracks, would be demolished within a matter of minutes. But time passed, and suddenly, after an hour, we saw the bazooka boys coming back toward us across the fields.

"My God," said Mydans, "they look as if the ball game was over and it's time to go home."

"What's going on?" I asked a sergeant.

"We ran out of ammo," he answered bitterly. "And the enemy infantry moving up way outnumbers us. Besides, these damn bazooks don't do any good against those heavy tanks—they bounce right off."

So, on the very first day of the war, we began to learn that the bazookas were no match for the Soviet tanks unless they scored a lucky hit from very close range. But even so it seemed incredible that we were going to pull back with enemy tanks still within our lines. I was gripped with a sense of unreality that followed me through most of the war. Reality, I guess, is just what we are accustomed to—and in Korea there was never time to become accustomed to anything.

Bad News

Incredible or not, it was clear enough as we returned to the command post that we Americans had not only been soundly defeated in our first skirmish but that a major retreat of our battalion would be forced. We simply had nothing with which to halt the tanks, and we were far too few to prevent the North Korean infantry from coming around our flanks. We hated to think what was happening to Colonel Smith's forward battalion.

But you soon learn, at a war front, to place events firmly in separate emotional compartments. There was absolutely nothing to be gained by thinking about Colonel Smith's situation. When we got back to battalion headquarters I think most of us tried to lock the door of the worry compartment and concentrate on immediate, material problems.

Dealing with Mud and Fleas

This was fairly easy for me that day, for a very simple reason. My first act, on getting out of the jeep at headquarters, was to slip and sprawl flat on my belly in a muddy rice paddy. Soaked and mud-caked, my consuming, immediate interest was the getting-dry department.

Lieutenant Payne came to my rescue. He found me some dry green fatigues and gallantly escorted me to an empty thatched hut where I changed. Next on the list of compelling interests was flea powder. I had been in agony all day, completely defenseless against as vicious an assault as fleadom ever made. A thick network of bites pocked my waist, thighs, and ankles. I hurried down to the medic's hut to beg for the little gray box of insecticide powder which was to be my most precious personal possession of the Korean war.

The Unreality of Death

I was talking to a Medical Corps sergeant when they brought in the body of Private Shadrick. His face was uncovered. As they carefully laid his body down on the bare boards of the shack I noticed that his face still bore an expression of slight surprise. It was an expression I was to see often among the soldier dead. The prospect of death had probably seemed as unreal to Private Shadrick as the entire war still seemed to me. He was very young indeed—his fair hair and frail build made him look far less than his nineteen years.

Someone went to look for a dry blanket for him, and just then the medic came back with the flea powder. He glanced at the body as he was handing me the gray box.

"What a place to die," he said.

A Young Korean Is Unknowingly Drafted

Chang Kil-yong (Mark Monahan)

In the following viewpoint, Mark Monahan talks about his experiences as a teenaged Korean named Chang Kil-yong. He tells how Communist officials came to his family's farm in North Korea and arrested his father as an "enemy of the people." He shares his and his mother's shock when they learned that the Chinese had entered the Korean War and that the Communists, who had left their village earlier, would be back soon. He explains he had no choice but to join the many others escaping to South Korea and laments the fact that he could not persuade his mother to go with him. He goes on to describe his experiences after he left home, including those as a member of a United Nations guerrilla force. Monahan is a retired US Marine lieutenant colonel and a professor at Yonsei University in South Korea and the University of Maryland–Asia.

SOURCE. Alan R. Millett, "The Teenage Guerrilla," *Their War for Korea: American, Asian, and European Combatants and Civilians, 1945–1953.* Potomac Books, Inc., 2002. Copyright © 2002 Potomac Books, Inc. All rights reserved. Reproduced by permission.

My family had lived for generations on the west coast of Hwanghae Province [North Korea] about ten miles from the town of Songhwa. The nearest big town was Changyon, another ten miles away. My father and grandfather were well-to-do farmers and landholders, real *yangban* [traditional land-holding rural men resistant to modernization] except that they had modern ideas. My grandfather was a Presbyterian elder, and my father always supported the local church by providing housing for the pastor who visited our village once a month. We lived a self-sufficient life on our farm, and we made some money from the rent and crops of our tenant farmers. In 1945 my father sent my older brother to school in Seoul [South Korea]. Soon after independence, however, Korean Communist officials, led by one of our tenant farmers named Lee, came to our home and arrested my father, who was then sentenced to five years in prison for being an "enemy of the people." That left my mother, a very determined woman, and me to run the family farm and business. Even under Communism we did all right while we waited for my father's release from prison.

Hopes of Liberation

The night before the Korean War began we had a heavy rain—thunder, lightning, the whole works. The next morning the air smelled as clean and fragrant as I've ever smelled it. The trees and flowers looked wonderful, suffused in light by the sun. But my mother and I heard this rumbling noise to the south. She said it must be the storm, but I could see no clouds and I didn't think she was right. Of course, what we heard was the tremendous artillery fire along the 38th Parallel [that roughly separates North and South Korea].

> At first the war meant nothing to us. Then Communist recruiting parties came to our village to find more soldiers.

At first the war meant nothing to us. Then Communist recruiting parties came to our village to find more soldiers. I thought I would not be taken since I was only fifteen, but by October you could tell that the Communists were desperate. We heard a rumor that the Communists were losing the war, and soon all political cadres [units] left our *myon* [territorial government unit similar to a US county]. We heard that the U.S. Army and the South Koreans would liberate us, so we held a great festival with the best food we had, and we went to church without any fear. We never saw a North Korean soldier or United Nations soldier in our village.

A Need to Leave Home

After the joy of liberation, the news that the Chinese had entered the war and that the Communists would soon return came as a great shock. Of course, the weather turned cold, and we had more snow than I had ever seen before. One day we heard the Communist soldiers were only five miles away, and I could see long lines of people struggling through the snow into the mountains along the coast. Someone had said that a South Korean ship was taking away anyone who wanted to flee the Communists. We also thought about fleeing south into South Korea. Mother gathered warm clothes, food, and blankets that we could carry, but she wanted to go into the mountains to wait for the return of the United Nations soldiers. I thought we'd better get the hell out while we had a chance, and that meant going to the coast or heading south. I knew that if I stayed I would be either shot as a "capitalist" or, more likely, drafted into the North Korean army. Mother refused to leave. She said she would wait for Father to be released from prison. I thought he would already have returned home if he was alive, and I wanted to get out.

I left her standing by our home and joined the stream of refugees trudging toward the coast. I don't know how

> There we learned we had just joined the South Korean army and that we would go to Cho-do Island for basic training.

many people I saw struggling through the snow, but it must have been thousands. When I finally reached the coast, I could see a South Korean ship, probably some sort of amphibious vessel, lying offshore just out of mortar range—and the Communists were trying to hit her. Small boats of all kinds, including fishing boats, were picking people up at the cliffs and taking them through the shellfire to the ship. I was amazed that the people remained so quiet except for calling out names to one another, but then someone said that the last boat had arrived. The crowd moaned. I just jumped from the cliff right on top of some guy, and we both tumbled on the deck. I had no intention of being stranded on the cliffs with the other people.

Joining the Military

The ship, of course, was a madhouse, packed with people and their pitiful belongings. There was very little food and water and too much crap. I have no idea how many people were aboard, but it had to be more than a thousand. After the ship got under way, some ROK [Republic of Korea] marines divided the refugees. All the old people, women, and children stayed aboard for the trip south to Pusan [South Korea], while the young men, maybe five hundred of us, transferred to another ship. There we learned we had just joined the South Korean army and that we would go to Cho-do Island for basic training. We would remain at military bases on the islands off the west coast of North Korea. After two or three weeks under the most primitive conditions we began military training, including shooting American weapons. We slept packed in an old schoolhouse and washed outside in the snow and cold. Then we went south to a bigger island, probably Paengnyong-do, to a larger military camp, where

down a dirt road that was the site of battles during the Korean War. The war brought an end to Chang Kil-yong's family farming tradition. (John Dominis/Time & Life Pictures/Getty Images.)

we organized companies according to where we came from in Hwanghae Province. I became a member of the White Tiger Unit of the 1st Partisan Infantry Regiment. Of course, we had no idea that we had become members of Army Unit 8240, the United Nations Partisan Forces, Korea, a guerrilla force modeled after the OSS [Office of Strategic Services] units of World War II. Our teams were code-named "Donkey," and then numbered. I think we were "Donkey Six." We did see our first U.S. soldiers at "Leopard Base," one of whom was black. The U.S. cadre at "Leopard" numbered around twenty-five. I had never seen a black man before, so I found his appearance amazing. We received uniforms—mostly U.S. Army castoffs—and weapons. I became a radioman on an AN/GRC-9, a radio we used to communicate with planes and ships, and I carried an M-2 carbine [rifle]. I really didn't work the radio, just pumped away at the hand-driven generator. I did what I was told. We had some very tough NCOs [non-commissioned officers], most of them from the Korean Marine Corps, so we didn't want to make them mad or they'd beat the crap out of us.

On Reconnaissance

I never did learn exactly what our mission was, but we made ten-day patrols into Hwanghae Province to learn what the Communists were doing. Some units raided enemy coastal outposts, but mine did reconnaissance work, which meant that we avoided all contact. At first we took food from the peasants, but they said that the Communists would kill them if they helped us, so my team leader said we would eat only what we could carry. Our food supply thus limited our area of operations. Basically, we tried to observe Communist troop movements and report them, so that U.N. aircraft or ships could attack targets along the roads south. Our leader was very cautious; we thought he was great. We never had a firefight, although other units did. I remember a friend of mine being all shot up with a burp gun. Some units just disappeared. My strongest memory is the smell of American C-rations cooking over a small fire. I never smelled food so good, and I ate all I could get my hands on. I had no idea I would eat so many Cs all over the world as an American Marine!

After the War

We stayed on our island bases until the armistice, when we finally went to South Korea. I took a discharge from the Army in 1954 as a sergeant because I wanted to go to school. I remember seeing the schoolboys in Seoul after the war, carrying books and wearing school uniforms, running to their classes. They were not much younger than I, but the war had cost me my teenage years and my education. After a try at attending a Presbyterian seminary for about a year, I went back to the Army. I didn't know anything except how to be a soldier. I never learned what happened to my mother, but my father escaped and came to Seoul. And I ended up in America.

A North Korean Officer Fights in the War

Lee Jong Kan

In the following viewpoint, Lee Jong Kan, an ethnic Korean from northeast China, relates how and why at age seventeen he signed on as a soldier in the Chinese Communist Army. He relates that his parents reacted negatively when he told them he wanted to join the army and what changed their minds about his decision. He describes his military career, which began with the Chinese fight against the Japanese, spanned the Chinese Civil War, and ended with the Korean War. He reveals what North Korean leader Kim Il Sung expected of the army even when it was in retreat. Lee Jong Kan provides insight from the Chinese and North Korean perspective into the conduct and battles of the Korean War in which he took part, including his battalion's last major battle—the defense of the South Korean capital of Seoul. Lee Jong Kan is a Chinese Communist Army veteran.

SOURCE. Richard Peters and Xiaobing Li, "A North Korean Officer's Story," *Voices from the Korean War: Personal Stories of American, Korean, and Chinese Soldiers.* University Press of Kentucky, 2004. Copyright © 2004 The University Press of Kentucky. All rights reserved. Reproduced by permission.

In 1928, I was born into a Korean farmer's family in Hailin County, Heilongjiang Province, Northeast China. . . . We are Chinese citizens, but we speak Korean, celebrate our holidays, and keep our traditions. . . .

A Reason to Join the Army

In the spring of 1945, a Chinese Communist Army recruiting team visited our village. They promised city employment for each Korean soldier at his retirement from the service. . . .

> 'You are only seventeen,' my mother yelled at me with tears in her eyes.

It seemed a good opportunity for me. To live in a city and use the knowledge I learned in my school was all I wanted. As a middle school graduate, I was considered a "degree-holder." . . . Listen to this, less than 20 percent of the Chinese people had a middle school diploma at that time. The war could help me move out of the countryside and land a job in the city. I was so excited after the meeting, I was ready to sign up.

But my parents said no. They had five boys. Three of them had already joined the CCP [Chinese Communist Party] armed forces, later called the People's Liberation Army (PLA). My parents still hadn't heard from them since they left home. My parents were so happy to see me coming back home to their farm. "You are only seventeen," my mother yelled at me with tears in her eyes. "Don't leave. You don't even know how to take care of yourself." . . .

My parents finally let me go when they learned that a large number of adult males in this Korean village had signed up, including my uncles and cousins. They felt even better when I told them that the Chinese Communist Army would keep us together in the same unit by organizing Korean companies, Korean battalions, and Korean regiments.

War Instead of Retirement

After two weeks of training in a Communist infantry training camp in Heilongjiang [province of northern China], I was assigned to the Forty-sixth Korean Regiment of the Sixteenth Division. My middle school education in my record surely caught the eyes of the regimental officers, who appointed me an assistant political instructor in the Seventh Company. . . .

The Pacific war suddenly ended on August 15, 1945. As a CCP member and a WWII vet, I thought I could retire from the army and get a city job.

I was wrong. The Chinese Civil War between the CCP and the KMT [Chinese Nationalist Party] broke out in 1946. Instead of demobilizing, the army fought another nationwide war, which continued until 1949. Our Korean regiment was enlarged into the 118th Korean Division, Fortieth Army, Fourth Field Army of the PLA. Our army fought the KMT troops all the way . . . from North China to the southern end of China, Hainan Island.

No Retirement Again

On October 1, 1949, Mao Zedong, CCP Chairman, announced the founding of the People's Republic of China (PRC) in Beijing, following the PLA forces' conquest of the mainland and the KMT's withdrawal to Taiwan Island. Finally, the Chinese Civil War was over. By the end of the year, I was promoted to battalion political commissar. I was looking forward to a more comfortable retirement and a better job in Guangzhou, the largest industrial and commercial city in South China. . . .

I was wrong again. When we were preparing a massive PLA demobilization in February 1950, we heard some rumors about the conflicts between North Korea and South Korea. In the North, the Korean Workers' Party, or the Korean Communist Party, had established a Communist state, the Democratic People's Republic of Korea (DPRK). In the South, the Korean Nationalists founded the Republic of Korea [ROK], Kim Il Sung, North Korea's Communist leader, wanted his fellow Communist Korean-Chinese soldiers back home to complete the Korean revolution. Kim intended to defeat South Korea's Nationalist army and extend his Communist regime over the entire Korean peninsula. . . .

Back Home Again to Prepare for Korea

In April, our Korean division received an order to leave Guangzhou and move all the way from the south to Northeast China. After a long railway trip, about twenty-five hundred miles, we were back home in Heilongjiang Province and prepared for a "return" to North Korea. I didn't know why they called it "return," since I had never been in Korea. Neither had most of the Korean soldiers in my battalion.

> Although I still served as a battalion political commissar, I was now ranked as a Korean army colonel.

My parents were so glad to see me when I visited them in May 1950. They were even happier to know I was going to Korea to fight my third war. Well, they believed the Korean War was not supposed to be a bloody one among the Korean people themselves. . . .

In June 1950, the Korean War broke out. . . .

A New Division, an Offensive Victory

On August 25, 1950, our division entered North Korea. There were two Korean divisions in the Chinese army, about fourteen thousand soldiers of Korean origin, both of which were transferred into the North Korean People's Army (NKPA). We kept our weapons and equipment, and the same formation, unit, and commanding officers when we were incorporated into the Thirty-third Regiment of the NKPA's Twenty-sixth Division. . . .

The NKPA, however, was a more Russianized army than the PLA. First of all, they had a Soviet officer ranking system that the Chinese did not have until 1955. Although I still served as a battalion political commissar, I was now ranked as a Korean army colonel. Second, their weapons and equipment were better than ours. Before the Red Army withdrew from North Korea, the Soviets re-armed the NKPA with Russian-made tanks, heavy artillery pieces, and automatic rifles, which we did not have. Our Korean comrades were so happy to see us entering the Korean War. . . .

In late August, our battalion participated in the NKPA's fourth offensive campaign. We broke the enemy defensive line and pushed ROK and UN [United Nations] troops into a small area east of the Naktong River in South Korea. By the end of the month, the NKPA had liberated 90 percent of the country and had control of 92 percent of the population.

The Last Offensive Campaign

On August 31, Kim launched his last offensive campaign against the enemy stronghold at Pusan. At that point, even though our troops' morale was high, the NKPA had suffered fifty-eight thousand casualties in its four southward offensive campaigns. It had also lost 120 of the 150 Russian-made tanks and one-third of its artillery pieces in the past two months. Most important, our transportation line had been extended more than two hundred miles. Our supply became more and more difficult. Our defense at the rear, if any, became weaker and weaker. . . . The faster we could win the last battle, the less opportunity the enemy had for a counterattack. However, we couldn't break the enemy defense at the Pusan perimeter during our offensive campaign.

After our failure at the Pusan perimeter, the NKPA could not launch another major offensive campaign. On September 10, we went on the defensive when the

ROK and UNF [United Nations Forces] launched their first major counteroffensive. Our situation became especially serious after [General Douglas] MacArthur landed twenty thousand U.S. troops at Inchon on September 15. We pulled out from the south and rushed back to the middle of the peninsula to defend Seoul, the capital city of the ROK, which had been occupied by the NKPA since June 28.

Seoul: Mobilizing the Citizens

The defense of Seoul on September 21–28 was our last major battle. I told my battalion that the NKPA had concentrated more than twenty thousand troops at Seoul, and that Comrade Kim was in the city with us. We had to stop the enemy offensive right here. Our battalion took up defensive positions in a tractor factory on the south side of the city. Our job was to stop any retreat from our front line and then reorganize a second defense.

> Our position was bombed and shelled heavily by superior UN air and artillery firepower.

I also remember that our Thirty-third Regiment Commissar recommended to other battalions my approach to a civilian mobilization. I held a meeting with about two hundred workers remaining in the factory and asked them: "Who are the Communist Party members?" "We are," they shouted, and about three dozen workers stood up. I asked them to join our defense. We showed the workers how to shoot and armed them with our extra rifles.

The NKPA mobilized the entire population in the city, even arming and training the women and children. NKPA-occupied Seoul was ready for its final battle.

Under Attack in Seoul

On September 21, MacArthur launched an all-out attack against Seoul. Our position was bombed and shelled heavily by superior UN air and artillery firepower. Instead of fighting, many factory workers dropped their weapons and left. I didn't stop them. Later that day, some NKPA soldiers began to withdraw from our first defense line, passing us and moving northward. I didn't stop them either. Most of them were wounded. Next evening, UN troops broke our first defense line.

About 4:00 A.M. on September 23, the enemy began to shell our position again. It was so heavy, I realized that the enemy troops were going to attack our second defense line soon. At 4:30, the enemy charged our position with about three hundred infantry troops led by ten light tanks. Our battalion commander ordered anti-tank teams to go out there one after another. But they couldn't stop the tanks. Some of the tanks ran over our trenches. We had to stop shooting and hide ourselves from tank firing power. We waited until the enemy troops came close and then opened fire. Some of my soldiers had a hand-to-hand fight. A few factory workers who stayed with us lit up several gasoline barrels and rolled these fireballs toward the tanks, finally stopping the tanks.

Time to Withdraw

After we defeated the enemy's second attack around 9:00 A.M., our commander called the Thirty-third Regiment Headquarters for reinforcement and supplies. We had lost half of our men. Many wounded needed medical care. We had almost run out of ammunition. But the Thirty-third Headquarters did not send anything. . . .

We managed to hold our position until 4:00 P.M., when we were ordered to withdraw after dark and "carry on our defense in the city." We left the factory about 9:00 in the evening, leaving many comrades' bodies behind.

Our fight in the streets of Seoul, which continued for three more days, was no longer an organized, effective defense. Kim and the NKPA Command had fled to the North, and our divisional and regimental communications had collapsed. We were pretty much on our own. Our men just tried to find a way to get out of there. The UN troops were well trained for a house-to-house battle. And the ROK troops were familiar with their capital city and its population. I was so surprised to see the same residents who warmly welcomed us a week before now welcome the ROK troops back into the city with cooked food and the ROK national flags.

Retreat—But Keep Fighting

During the night of September 27, the battalion commander, two of his staff, six soldiers, and I broke through the enemy lines and headed north, through the woods. We had no radio, no ammunition, and no food.

> According to the new order, we would fight on our own behind the lines by harassing the enemy troops, attacking their communication and transportation, and recruiting for the NKPA.

Fortunately, we ran into the NKPA Twenty-seventh Regiment . . . two days later. By that time, we also heard Kim's new policy, issued on September 27 to all the North Korean troops, party members, and people. Our new task was to slow down the enemy offensive, save the main part of the NKPA, organize a strategic withdrawal, and build up a new reserve for a future counteroffensive.

The NKPA defense was put to rout all along the line by the end of September. We retreated north all the way to Pyongyang, the capital city of North Korea. After a one-week defense, the UNF took over Pyongyang on October 19. There was not much room left in North Korea for our further withdrawal.

Some of our soldiers thought we might pull out and go back to China. Kim, however, wouldn't let us go. After Pyongyang fell, we were ordered to break up the battalion into several guerrilla groups. According to the new order, we would fight on our own behind the lines by harassing the enemy troops, attacking their communication and transportation, and recruiting for the NKPA.

An End to Suffering and Battle

As a group leader, I led fifty men to the eastern coast and established a small base in a mountain. We hit and ran at night and rested in the daytime. Without any supplies and local connections, we had to hunt small animals to feed ourselves and capture enemy ammunition and medical supplies for our needs. That winter (1950–1951) in Korea was extremely cold. We didn't even have winter clothes, blankets, or tents. Some of our comrades survived the battles but did not make it through the long, cold winter.

Finally, we were able to move off of the mountain in April 1951. . . . We were recognized back into NKPA regulars in May 1951.

But I could no longer keep up with my unit in the night because of my poor sight. I got night blindness due to the lack of nutrition and medicine during our mountainous guerrilla warfare. I was sent back to China for treatment in the summer of 1951.

After a few weeks in a PLA hospital, I was retired from the NKPA first, and then from the PLA as a disabled war veteran. An officer asked me in his office where I wanted to retire to, China or North Korea? "Here, China, of course," I told him without even thinking about it. China is my homeland, and the war was still going on in Korea.

An American Doctor Serves in Korea

Otto F. Apel, Jr., and Pat Apel

In the following viewpoint, Otto F. Apel, Jr., recalls his experiences as a doctor serving in a mobile army surgical hospital (MASH) during the Korean War. He details the primitive living conditions they had to put up with, including brutal cold; mud and dust everywhere; old army cots and sleeping bags; latrines that offered little or no privacy; and ever-present mosquitoes, flies, and rats. He goes on to describe his unit's favorite place to go whenever they could squeeze in some time to relax, to swim, sunbathe, play volleyball, and enjoy the Korean countryside. Otto F. Apel, Jr., served as a surgeon during the Korean War and was a consultant to the *MASH* television series. His son and co-author, Pat Apel, is an attorney.

SOURCE. Otto F. Apel, Jr., and Pat Apel, "Where We Lived," *MASH: An Army Surgeon in Korea*. University Press of Kentucky, 1998. Copyright © 1998 The University Press of Kentucky. All rights reserved. Reproduced by permission.

Korea was a young person's war. In 1950 the cadre of the army was left over from World War II and, like the army's equipment, had aged markedly in a few years. The officers and commanders at the beginning of the war were, by army standards, quite seasoned. Gen. Douglas MacArthur hovered near seventy at the time of the Inchon invasion [in Korea]. Maj. Gen. Edward "Ned" Almond, MacArthur's chief of staff, was fifty-eight years old. Gen. Walton Harris Walker, commander of the U.S. Eighth Army at the outbreak of hostilities, was born in 1889. Down through the corps, divisions, regiments, and battalions, the commanders and staff personnel were, in 1950, older than their counterparts have been in any other war. But the people drafted to fill the ranks, as in many other wars, were the young from the schools and the streets of the civilian world.

> The war moved, the MASH moved, we moved, and in all that mobility the war, the MASH, and we, individually, changed and continued to change.

The Medical Corps was no different. The rank and file doctors and nurses had been discharged after World War II, leaving behind only a skeleton crew of the white-haired battalion. After the doctors' draft, the new rank and file of the Medical Corps hailed directly from the medical schools, the nursing schools, and the teaching hospitals of the United States. As I looked around, I saw doctors and nurses, lieutenants, captains, and majors who were new not only to the army but also to the profession of medicine. . . .

The MASH: Not an Easy Life

We were busy. The war moved, the MASH [mobile army surgical hospital] moved, we moved, and in all that mobility the war, the MASH, and we, individually, changed and continued to change. The best way to put it into perspective perhaps is to think of the changes you would have to make if you knew that for the next year all the aspects of your life, eating, sleeping, bathing, were to be in a tent, that the temperatures would swing from zero to well over one hundred, that you would walk on muddy roads, ride in trucks without shocks, sleep in crowded quarters, and never find a solitary moment, and all that in the middle of a war. . . .

Living conditions in MASH 8076 were rudimentary at best. Water, a necessity often taken for granted, had to be carried with the unit by water truck. Drinking water was a precious commodity. We filled canteens and buckets and steel pots (the army helmet) from the water truck. We dared not drink out of streams or lakes for fear of what the North Koreans or the Chinese may have done to them. All personnel lived in tents and used portable showers or cans of heated water to wash and orange crates for bedside tables and makeup desks. . . . Mud or dust was everywhere. A trip from tent to tent gathered cakes of mud on the bottoms of shoes and deposited the mud on the floors.

Bedding: Making Do

We considered our bedding a luxury because it was much better than what the soldiers at the front used: the army sleeping bag. Bedding was most often the old army cot with army blankets and linens. A modern convenience was a small mattress that fit on the cot and made sleeping a little easier. On one occasion MASH 8055 lost all its mattresses and sheets when someone flipped a cigarette into the truck carrying the bedding during a tactical move. They had to go without linens and bedding until they could be replaced through army supply channels. For several weeks the army sleeping bag had to suffice. There were times, however, when the sleeping bag was the bedding of choice. In the brutal cold of the Korean winter, the nurses slept in long johns, flannel pajamas covered by a sweater, stockings, gloves, an operating room stockinette on their head, and anything else they could find and pull on. Thus prepared, they slipped inside a sleeping bag and pulled up several layers of blankets.

Latrines, Not Bathrooms

The latrine [lavatory] was little more than a slit trench surrounded by blankets draped between stakes for privacy. It constantly needed cleaning and disinfecting. When we had been in one place for a while, the enlisted personnel would build a multihole wooden toilet over the trench for comfort and convenience. In the cold weather, the latrines created an updraft that was unbearable. Soon after the Korean winter came, each sleeping tent was equipped with one large galvanized iron bucket that sat in a dark corner. Even in warm weather, using the latrine could be hazardous. Two operating room nurses from the 8076th went to the latrine together. The weather was sunny, but the clouds raced by and the wind gusted. Suddenly, a blast of wind caught the blankets, and away they sprawled across the field, dragging the stakes behind them. The two nurses, to their great embarrassment, sat on the wooden toilet in the middle of the open field in broad daylight.

> The latrines . . . were breeding grounds for the scourges of Korea: flies and rats.

The latrines had to be cared for constantly. Though they began as slit trenches, they were upgraded as time allowed. They were breeding grounds for the scourges of Korea: flies and rats. In the summer months flies were everywhere. They were not flies like we have in the United States. These were the large green kind that buzz with the ferocity of a Russian MIG [fighter plane]. Constant cleaning of the mess hall, burial or burning of garbage and hospital waste materials, placement of latrines, and use of [the toxic insecticide] DDT kept the

Performing lifesaving operations in a battle zone was only one of the many challenges faced by mobile army surgical hospital personnel in Korea. (Transcendental Graphics/Getty Images.)

flies down to a minimum for part of the time. Fly screens and screen doors were mandatory on all tents during the summer months. The facilities and incoming personnel were dusted with DDT on a regular basis. . . .

Dealing with Mosquitoes, Rats, and the Dark

These measures were aimed at flies but worked for mosquitoes also. DDT checked the spread of malaria so that in 1951 we had only twelve malaria cases—half of those were members of our command. An active campaign against malaria cranked up in the spring and lasted into December. Each person was required to take a daily dose of chloroquine. Two of the 8076th personnel who contracted malaria admitted that they had not taken their regular doses.

Rats were also a common presence in Korea. Control was difficult because of our temporary conditions and facilities and because of the destruction brought by the war. Rats are a symptom of combat. Cleanliness and garbage control, both very difficult in field conditions, were the chief weapons used against this nuisance. . . . We used traps and poison to keep the rat population under control. In addition, we placed bricks on the floors of our tents, which kept the floors drier and prevented some of the conditions in which rats proliferated. Even with these efforts, rats managed to explore nearly everything we had. An unexpected scream from a doctor or a nurse was, in all likelihood, caused by the opening of a storage box to find a field rat jumping about.

All of our walkways in the MASH were lined with white rocks. The Koreans did that everywhere we went. As soon as the tents went up, the rocks came out and the paths were marked off. At first we smiled about this practice and wondered whether it was a quaint Korean cultural condition: the need to line every path with small white rocks. The first time we went outside a tent at night, however, we learned the utility of white rocks. In blackout conditions it was pitch dark at night. We carried small flashlights, more like penlights, and they had just enough power to illuminate the white rocks so that we could see the paths. . . .

The MASH Nurses

Seventeen nurses were assigned to MASH 8076. The nurses stayed together in a large sleeping tent they dubbed Whispering Manor. I do not recall the exact origin of that term, but it was an apt term because the

> "Older women—and men—would have had to be in exceptional physical condition to stand the stress of the living conditions and the strain of the working conditions in the MASH."

"manor," it seemed, was always whispering about something. The nurses' tent was off limits to male personnel because there were always nurses in the tent sleeping or relaxing (they worked rotations in the various sections). It would never dawn on any of us that someone might go into Whispering Manor uninvited. Yet on two occasions in 1951 the tent, with nurses asleep inside, was broken into at night by burglars, who stole personal items. The burglars were never caught, but after that we all kept a sharper eye out around the MASH.

All the nurses were young. That was one of the prerequisites of serving in the MASH. Granted, it forfeited the experience of the older nurses. But older women—and men—would have had to be in exceptional physical condition to stand the stress of the living conditions and the strain of the working conditions in the MASH. . . .

Relaxing at the Hwachon Reservoir

Each time we had the opportunity—and there were not many such times—we relaxed. There were times when we stopped for a drink and laughed as we talked of home and life without the war. Our best place, ironically, was at the Hwachon Reservoir in the fall of 1951. We moved north above the thirty-eighth parallel in the United Nations counteroffensive in the late summer of 1951 and located the MASH on the east end of the Hwachon Reservoir, a huge body of water nearly twenty miles in length. The fighting . . . was to the north of the reservoir. It was extremely hot that summer, often over one hundred degrees, and the fighting was very heavy. We found a place not far from the MASH where the river emptied into the reservoir. The river made a large bend, and the inside bank of the bend was a sandy beach.

Shortly after we settled into our encampment, we rigged a barbecue grill on the riverbank and slipped away in the late afternoons to swim and sunbathe. It was a delightful spot where we could relax and enjoy the beauty of the Korean countryside. The pilots and the NCOs [non-commissioned officers], who were excellent scroungers, managed to bring supplies of beer and steaks and hamburgers and hot dogs; we would crank up the grills and cook in the summer afternoons. All of us, doctors and nurses, managed to find bathing suits. Several of the nurses had two-piece suits, which were the rage stateside.

> " Shortly after we settled into our encampment, we rigged a barbecue grill on the riverbank and slipped away in the late afternoons to swim and sunbathe. "

Enjoying the Moment

Eventually we built a rickety diving platform on the bank and found some old rubber inner tubes. We rigged several boards near the bank as a dock for those less adventurous sorts who would not brave the diving platform. The Koreans came to the watering hole also and swam with us. . . . We put up an improvised volleyball net, and everyone played, doctors, nurses, enlisted personnel, pilots, Koreans, ambulance drivers—everyone who wanted to play could play.

Sometimes the pilots would send the young Koreans up the river with empty beer cans to toss into the current so they would bob down to where we were. The pilots would target practice with their sidearms. . . . They enjoyed teaching the nurses how to shoot. Most of the nurses were eager to learn, if only to spend some time in recreation with the pilots. On other occasions the pilots would take the nurses up in the helicopters to view the beauty of the reservoir and the beach from the air. Eventually everyone, including . . . Korean civilians, took pleasure rides in the helicopters.

A Black Cloud over Paradise

The beach, by all appearances, had the potential for one of those isolated South Sea island experiences: young men and women, far from home, tied to a postcard-pretty location. In fact, some of the men and women did become interested in one another. After the war, the commander of the ambulance platoon married one of the nurses he met in the 8076th. But our "paradise" was like picnicking at the beach with a huge black cloud approaching on the horizon. No matter how comfortable it became on that beach, we were always glancing at our big black cloud, the omnipresent threat of combat. At any time we could get the call; the helicopters, forewarning us, would rev up, take to the skies, and return with the wounded. Regardless of the circumstances, we could leave whatever we were doing at the beach and be in the operating room ready to receive patients within two minutes. When the fighting began, it was like cramming everything into the picnic basket and running when the bottom dropped out of the big black cloud and you had to sprint for cover to get out of the rain and thunder and lightning.

A Korean Family Suffers the Hardships of War

Lee Hyun Sook

In the following viewpoint, a Korean woman recalls the hardships endured by her family and others as they fled their homes in the South Korean city of Seoul in 1950 to escape its occupation by North Korean troops. She tells how the hopefulness she and her family felt when they arrived in the city of Hong Song to live with her husband's brother turned quickly to fear when the North Koreans arrived. She speaks of her husband's patriotism and describes what happened to him when, after hiding out from the North Koreans, he was caught and arrested for supporting South Korea. Lee Hyun Sook, a housewife and mother who lived with her family in Seoul, South Korea, at the time of the Korean War, came in 1985 to the United States, where she went into business with her daughter.

SOURCE. Richard Peters and Xiaobing Li, "A Korean Housewife's Story," *Voices from the Korean War: Personal Stories of American, Korean, and Chinese Soldiers*. University Press of Kentucky, 2004. Copyright © 2004 The University Press of Kentucky. All rights reserved. Reproduced by permission.

At the beginning of the Korean War in 1950, I lived in Seoul with my husband, Lee J. Won, and our nearly two-year-old daughter, Lee Hong Im. I was twenty-four years old at the time, and I stayed home to take care of the house and my little girl. My husband had an office job working for the electric department in Seoul.

At the time, we knew there were big problems between South and North Korea. Sometimes we heard about shootings around the 38th Parallel, which divided the two Koreas. We also knew that sometimes those living in North Korea crossed the Han River by boat to get into South Korea. Some even paid money to cross the river.

Escape to Hong Song

The North Koreans attacked on June 25 [1950], early in the morning. I was home and first heard the news on the radio. At that time most people had very little money or food, because it was near the end of the month, but we knew we still had to leave before the North Koreans arrived in Seoul. Fortunately, every day I had saved a handful of rice, so we had some food to take with us on our journey to the South.

> After we had been in Hong Song only about two days, the North Koreans arrived, and our lives were changed forever.

Together with my sister and her family, we crossed the Han River on a boat, with my husband carrying the bag of rice. Unfortunately, my sister was not a very healthy person, and she had several small children so we could only walk about ten miles a day. We walked for about fifteen days to Hong Song, a city about seventy miles south of Seoul near the West Coast. We chose Hong Song because this is where my husband's family lived. There were many others trying to escape the North Koreans, and some became so weak from lack of food they dropped out along the way and died. We saw many dead people on the way to Hong Song. Because we had some rice, we were okay. We even had some rice left over when we finally arrived in Hong Song.

An Atmosphere of Fear

Everything seemed so peaceful when we entered the city, and we were quite hopeful. We lived with my husband's family, and everything seemed to be okay. Then, after we had been in Hong Song only about two days, the North Koreans arrived, and our lives were changed forever.

Because he loved his country so much, in Hong Song my husband belonged to a local patriotic society. He received no pay, but sometimes gave the local police information on those who supported the North Koreans. The North Koreans, however, regularly arrested and put in jail anyone they suspected of supporting South Korea.

To stay out of jail, my husband and some of his friends hid in the basement of his older brother, Lee Chang Won, who lived in a very big house in Hong Song. He was an important official in the South Korean government, and sometimes he would hide as many as fifty people at one time in his basement.

At this time it was very difficult to know who to trust because there were many people in the South who welcomed the North Koreans, especially in the early part of the war. The North Koreans made Communism sound so wonderful that many thought it must be like heaven. It seemed to have a special appeal for both those with very little education and those with a lot of education. Many college students supported the North Koreans, especially those who studied in Japan.

Police Brutality and Intervention by a Friend

While my husband's older brother was very helpful to those who were wanted by the North Koreans, and

> We went down to the police station and found my husband so badly beaten he was near death.

hid many of them in his basement, he had a friend who supported the North Koreans and who became an important head man in the North Korean police. Even so, he didn't interfere with my family as long as we all stayed out of sight and caused no problems.

Unfortunately, one day my husband got tired of his basement hideout and decided to walk around outside. He was seized by the North Korean police, who brutally beat him up. When the friend of my husband's brother learned what happened, he came to our house and took my husband to the police station.

That night my husband never came home. I went to see my husband's brother to see if he knew what happened. Together, we went down to the police station and found my husband so badly beaten he was near death. His clothes were so soaked in blood they stuck to his skin when removed. When the head policeman, the friend of my husband's brother, learned what happened he made sure my husband received medical attention. Then he permitted my husband to go home. Without his help, I'm quite sure my husband would have died.

In Hiding from the North Koreans

While my husband continued to suffer terribly from the beatings, it was no longer safe for him to remain in our house. Fortunately, the friend of my husband's brother understood this. So late one night he came to our house and took my husband to another house about five miles away, where he could hide more safely.

My husband stayed in this house for several months, almost like a dead person. During the day he had to be very quiet and could hardly move. At first he still could not walk, but at night he exercised with a rope, and he built up his strength until he could walk again. Eventually, however, even this house became too dangerous for him to stay. So, with some other South Koreans who were wanted by the North Korean police, my husband and the others moved into the mountains, where they all lived in a cave.

Many of those who hid from the North Koreans were the former leaders of South Korea, often professional people with a college education. The North Koreans especially disliked these people and treated them with great cruelty. I know of one occasion when the North Koreans gathered about twenty to thirty of these people in a large building, then closed the door and gave each a good beating. Then they gave shovels to each person and led them into nearby mountains. After they had all dug a hole with their shovels, the North Koreans tied their hands behind their backs and shot them beside the holes. They just toppled over and fell into the holes all by themselves.

Life after the North Koreans Are Driven Out

My husband and his friends remained hidden in the mountains about two months, until the UN [United Nations] forces drove the Communist forces back into North Korea. When they finally emerged from their cave they were angry toward all of those who had worked for the North Koreans, and they tried to make sure they were arrested and sent to jail.

Gradually, my husband recovered from the beatings by the North Korean police. He spent the rest of the war in the South Korean army, although he was restricted to light duty because of his injuries. My daughter and I continued to live in Hong Song with my husband's family until the war ended and he returned from the army in 1953. Then we all went back to Seoul, to the same house, which somehow had survived all the fighting. My husband went back to his old job in the electric department, but unfortunately he died in 1958. Since my daughter eventually married an American serviceman from Oklahoma, in 1985 I came to Oklahoma.

GLOSSARY

CCP	Chinese Communist Party; ruling party of China.
Cold War	Attempt after World War II by the Soviet Union and the United States to gain world influence by means short of total war.
DPRK	Democratic People's Republic of Korea; North Korea.
Formosa	Island nation also known as Taiwan and, after 1949, the Republic of China; home to Nationalist Chinese.
Guomindang	Nationalist Party of China; ruling party of the Republic of China. Also romanized Kuomintang (KMT).
KGB	Committee for State Security; Soviet intelligence agency.
McCarthyism	Public allegation of disloyalty to one's country, especially through pro-Communist activity, often without proof or based on slight, doubtful, or irrelevant evidence; term created in 1950 by cartoonist Herb Block referring to the actions and activities of Senator Joseph McCarthy.
MIGs	Russian fighter jets.
Myon	North Korean administrative unit; township.
NATO	North Atlantic Treaty Organization; military alliance of democratic states in North America and Europe.
NSC-68	National Security Council Report 68; classified report issued in 1950 that for 20 years shaped US government actions in the Cold War.
PLA	People's Liberation Army; China's military organization, made up of land, sea, and air forces.

Red	Communist.
POWs	Prisoners of war.
ROK	Republic of Korea; South Korea.
Taipeh	Capital of Taiwan.
38th parallel	Latitudinal line that more or less forms the boundary between North Korea and South Korea.
"two Chinas"	People's Republic of China (PRC), or Communist China, which controls mainland China, Hong Kong, and Macau; and Republic of China (ROC), or Nationalist China, which controls the island nation of Taiwan and some nearby island groups.
United Nations (UN)	International organization of independent states formed in 1945 to promote international peace and security and economic development.
UNO	United Nations Organization; United Nations.
USSR	Union of Soviet Socialist Republics; commonly known as the Soviet Union.
Yangban	Part of the traditional ruling class or nobles of premodern Korea who were in essence administrators and bureaucrats.

CHRONOLOGY

1950 June 25: North Korea crosses the 38th parallel and invades South Korea.

June 26: The United Nations (UN) Security Council calls for an immediate end to hostilities and for North Korea to withdraw its troops from South Korea.

June 27: President Harry S. Truman commits US naval and air support to South Korea. The United States asks the UN to provide assistance to South Korea to restore international peace. The UN calls for its members to support South Korea.

June 28: The South Korean capital of Seoul falls to the North Korean army.

June 30: President Truman commits US troops to enforce the United Nations demand.

July 7: The UN Security Council creates a new United Nations Command to be headed by US general Douglas MacArthur.

September 15: UN forces headed by General MacArthur launch an amphibious assault at Inchon.

September 29: General MacArthur and South Korean president Syngman Rhee enter Seoul and restore the Rhee government.

September 30: The first UN forces cross the 38th

Parallel. China warns it will intervene if UN forces advance farther north.

October 19: South Korean and US troops capture the North Korean capital of Pyongyang. Chinese Communist forces cross the Yalu River into North Korea to provide support of that country.

1951   January 1: The North Korean and Chinese offensive gets underway.

January 3: UN forces abandon Seoul.

March 18: UN forces take back Seoul.

April 11: President Truman dismisses General MacArthur. General Matthew Ridgway replaces MacArthur.

June 23: The Soviet ambassador to the UN proposes truce talks.

July 10: Truce talks get underway at the North Korean border town of Kaesong.

August 23: The Communists break off the truce talks.

October 25: Truce talks get underway again at Panmunjom inside the Demilitarized Zone.

November 27: Truce talks continue at Panmunjom and agreement is reached on a cease-fire line.

1952   January 2: The UN submits a proposal for a prisoner of war (POW) exchange.

January 3: The Communists reject the UN POW

exchange proposal.

May 12: General Mark Clark becomes the new commander of the United Nations Command (UNC).

July 11: The first strike is made on the North Korean capital of Pyongyang.

August 29: The second strike is made on the North Korean capital of Pyongyang.

October 8: Truce talks are recessed for an indefinite period of time.

November 4: Dwight Eisenhower is elected president of the United States.

1953 March 5: Soviet leader Joseph Stalin dies.

April 26: Truce talks get underway again.

June 8: The POW issue is settled.

June 16: The first cease-fire is concluded.

June 18: 25,000 North Korean prisoners of war are released. Communists break off truce talks again.

July 10: Truce talks resume again.

July 27: The armistice is signed by the Communists and the UNC.

September 23: Repatriation of POWs gets underway at Panmunjom.

1968 January 21: North Korean commandos unsuccessfully

attempt to assassinate South Korean president Park Chung-Hee.

1987   November 29: A bomb planted on a South Korean airplane by agents of North Korea explodes killing everyone on board.

1991   June 15: The first naval battle between North Korea and South Korea since the Korean War takes place along the Yellow Sea border.

2002   June 29: A South Korean ship is sunk when the two Koreas clash along the Yellow Sea border.

2009   November 10: North and South Korean navies exchange fire near the Yellow Sea border.

2010   March 26: An unexplained explosion sinks the South Korean warship *Cheonan* near the maritime border with North Korea, resulting in the death of 46 sailors.

May 20: A report released by a multinational investigation team indicates that a North Korean torpedo sunk the *Cheonan*.

May 24: South Korea suspends trade with North Korea and bans its ships from Seoul's waters.

October 29: North and South Korean troops exchange fire across their border.

November 23: North Korea fires artillery shells onto a South Korean border island, resulting in an exchange of fire, fatalities, and property damage and leading South Korea to put its military on the highest non-wartime alert.

December 28: South Korean president Lee Myung-bak warns that South Korea will "respond relentlessly" to further attacks by North Korea.

FOR FURTHER READING

Books

Clay Blair, *The Forgotten War: America in Korea, 1950–1953.* New York: Times Books, 1987.

James Brady, *The Scariest Place in the World: A Marine Returns to North Korea.* New York: Thomas Dunne Books, 2005.

Commander Eugene Franklin Clark, *The Secrets of Inchon: The Untold Story of the Most Daring Covert Mission of the Korean War.* New York: Berkley Publishing Group, 2002.

Bruce Cumings, *The Korean War.* New York: Modern Library, 2010.

David Douglas Duncan, *This Is War!: A Photo-Narrative of the War.* Boston: Little, Brown and Company, 1990.

Donald M. Goldstein, *The Korean War: The Story and Photographs.* Washington: Brassey's, 2001.

Linda Granfield, *I Remember Korea: Veterans Tell Their Stories of the Korean War, 1950–53.* New York: Clarion Books, 2003.

Max Hastings, *The Korean War.* New York: Simon & Schuster Paperbacks, 1987.

Michael Hickey, *The Korean War: The West Confronts Communism.* Woodstock, NY: Overlook Press, 2000

Korean Institute of Military History, *The Korean War, Volume I–III.* Lincoln: The University of Nebraska Press, 2001.

Bong Lee, *The Unfinished War.* New York: Algora Publishing, 2004.

Chi Young Pak, *Korea and the United Nations.* The Hague: Kluwer Law International, 2000.

Rod Paschall, *Witness to War: Korea.* New York: A Perigee Book Published by The Berkley Publishing Group, 1995.

Stanley Sandler, *The Korean War: No Victors, No Vanquished*. Lexington: The University Press of Kentucky, 1999.

Harry Spiller, *American POWs in Korea: Sixteen Personal Accounts*. Jefferson, NC: McFarland & Company, Inc., Publishers, 1998.

James L. Stokesbury, *A Short History of the Korean War*. New York: William Morrow and Company, 1988.

William Stueck, *Rethinking the Korean War: A New Diplomatic and Strategic History*. Princeton: Princeton University Press, 2002.

John Toland, *In Mortal Combat, Korea, 1950–1953*. New York: Morrow, 1991.

Charles Whiting, *Battleground Korea: The British in Korea*. Stroud, United Kingdom: Sutton Pub Ltd., 2003.

Arthur W. Wilson and Norman L. Strickbine, *Korean Vignettes: Faces of War: 201 Veterans of the Korean War Recall That Forgotten War Their Experiences and Thoughts and Wartime Photographs of That Era*. Portland, OR: Artwork Publications, 1996.

Periodicals

Captain B.R. Brinley, "Quiet Day at Panmunjom," *Harper's Magazine*, September 1953.

David Carter, "The Korean War at 60 Part Two: The Course of the War and the British Involvement," *Contemporary Review*, Autumn 2010.

Robert Dallek, "Wrong Turns in Korea," *American Heritage Magazine*, Fall 2010.

David Douglas Duncan, "U.S. Gets into Fight for Korea: An Eyewitness Report in Words and Pictures," *Life*, July 10, 1950.

Zhou Ming Fu, "My American Prisoner," *New York Times*, June 24, 2010.

Merrill Goozner, "The Legacy of the Korean War: Cold War Thinking Framed By Conflict," *Chicago Tribune*, July 25, 1993.

Walter Karp, "Truman vs. MacArthur," *American Heritage Magazine*, April–May 1984.

Andrei Lankov, "If the North Had Won the Korean War," *Asia Times*, September 8, 2007.

Christina Larson, "What's It Like to Be a Tourist in North Korea," *Foreign Policy*, August 16, 2010.

Eric Longabardi, Kit R. Roane, and Edward T. Pound, "A War of Memories," *U.S. News & World Report*, November 3, 2003.

Tom O'Neill, "Korea's DMZ: Dangerous Divide," *National Geographic*, July 2003.

Matthew B. Ridgway and Harold H. Martin, "My Battles in War and Peace: Conclusion: The Korean War," *Saturday Evening Post*, February 25, 1956.

"Soviet Blames Seoul and Its Backers for Starting Strife," *Washington Post*, June 30, 1950.

Douglas Stanglin and Peter Cary, "Secrets of the Korean War," *U.S. News & World Report*, June 9, 1993.

Thomas Walkom, "North Korea's Unending War Rages On," *Toronto Star*, November 25, 2010.

"War: Korea: Three Years of War," *Time*, June 29, 1953.

Kathryn Weathersby, "The Korean War Revisited," *The Wilson Quarterly*, Summer 1999.

Stanley Weintraub, "How to Remember the Forgotten War," *American Heritage*, May–June 2000.

Sheryl WuDunn, "Panmunjom Journal; For North Korea Still, the Americans Started It," *New York Times*, August 12, 1989.

Mun Yol Yi, "The Country America Cannot See," *New York Times*, July 27, 2003.

Websites

Korea+ 50: No Longer Forgotten (http://eisenhower.archives .gov/Research/Digital_Documents/Korea/Koreawar.html). This site is a joint project of the Harry S. Truman and Dwight D. Eisnhower Presidential Libraries and provides access to primary sources such as documents and photographs relating to the Korean War.

Korean War (www.history.com/topics/korean-war). This site provides articles, video and audio clips, photos, and facts about the Korean War, with a strong focus on the United States and its role in the war.

Korean War National Museum (www.theforgottenvictory.org). This site provides an image gallery, Korean War-related facts and statistics, and a listing of books on the war, as well as information on Korean veterans, reunions, and unit histories.

INDEX